This book belongs to

_____

_____

_____

D0624451

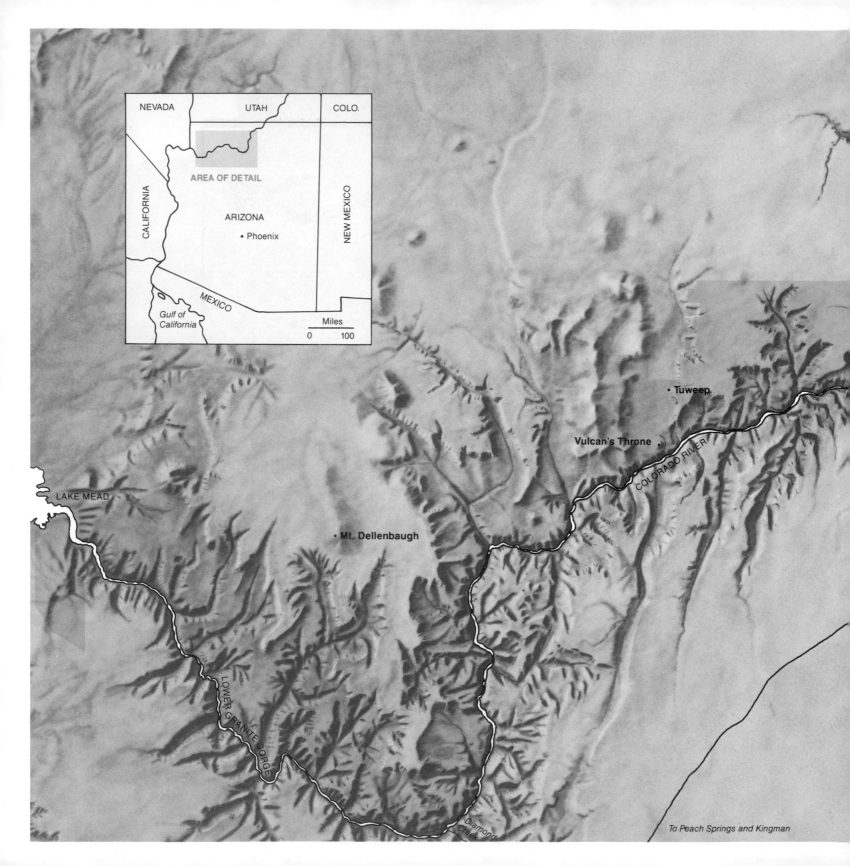

NEVADA   UTAH   COLO.

AREA OF DETAIL

CALIFORNIA

ARIZONA

• Phoenix

NEW MEXICO

MEXICO

Gulf of
California

Miles

0   100

LAKE MEAD

• Tuweep

Vulcan's Throne

COLORADO RIVER

• Mt. Dellenbaugh

LOWER GRANITE GORGE

Diamond
Creek

To Peach Springs and Kingman

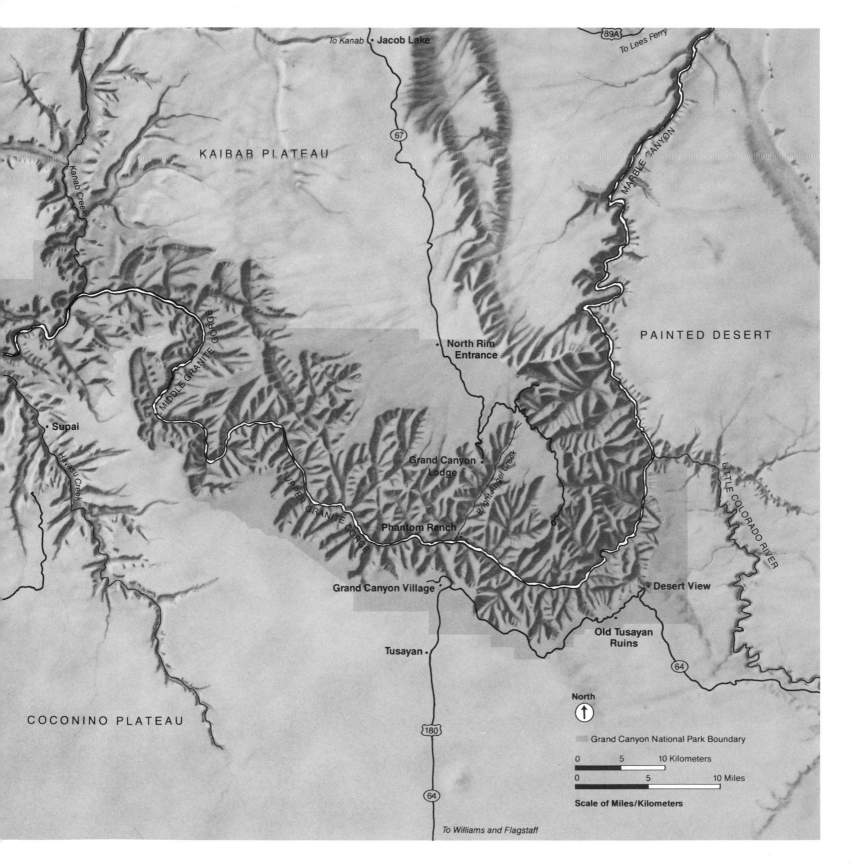

To Kanab • **Jacob Lake**

To Lees Ferry

89A

KAIBAB PLATEAU

67

Kanab Creek

MARBLE CANYON

PAINTED DESERT

MIDDLE GRANITE GORGE

• **North Rim Entrance**

• **Supai**

Havasu Creek

UPPER GRANITE GORGE

Grand Canyon Lodge

Bright Angel Creek

LITTLE COLORADO RIVER

Phantom Ranch

• **Desert View**

Grand Canyon Village •

Old Tusayan Ruins

Tusayan •

64

COCONINO PLATEAU

180

North

↑

Grand Canyon National Park Boundary

0   5   10 Kilometers

0   5   10 Miles

Scale of Miles/Kilometers

64

To Williams and Flagstaff

For Philip and Anna,
two of my favorite
Grand Canyon explorers.

EXPLORING THE GRAND CANYON:

Adventures of Yesterday and Today

Illustrations copyright © 1990 by the Grand Canyon Natural History Association
P.O. Box 399, Grand Canyon, Arizona 86023

Paperbound edition
ISBN 0-938216-33-3

Library of Congress number: 90-80128

EDITORIAL: Pamela Frazier
BOOK DESIGN: Diane Goldsmith
PRODUCTION: Square Moon Productions
TYPOGRAPHY: Dharma Enterprises
LITHOGRAPHY: Lorraine Press
COVER: Margaret Sanfilippo

ACKNOWLEDGEMENTS

PHOTOS: Page 31, Norman Fox; 38, Denver Public Library, Western History
Department. Drawing by Frederic Remington; 40, Sharlot Hall Historical Society;
42, Engraving by W. Woodruff from Pattie's *Narrative;* 45, Neg. #19735, Courtesy
Department of Library Services, American Museum of Natural History. Painting
by William Cary; 48, 50, 52, Engravings from *The Exploration of the Colorado
River and Its Canyons,* by J.W. Powell, Dover Press; 74, "Chasm of the Colorado"
by Thomas Moran, Courtesy of National Museum of American Art, Smithsonian
Institution; 113(T), R.S. Leding; 115, D.C. Ochsner; 117(T), 119, George H.H. Huey.

All other photos used by permission of the Grand Canyon National Park.

ILLUSTRATIONS: Pam Frazier, 141–142; Lloyd Goldsmith, 1, 7, 12–18, 23, 25, 29,
30, 37, 57, 71, 73, 83, 97.

All other illustrations by Margaret Sanfilippo.

EXPLORING THE GRAND CANYON:

Adventures of Yesterday and Today

by Lynne Foster

illustrated by Margaret Sanfilippo

Grand Canyon Natural History Association

CONTENTS

CONTENTS

The Grand Canyon, like the rest of our planet, is a happening, not a finished product. Like you and me, it has a life history, a past, and a future. To tell the Grand Canyon's story in an understandable way, we need to begin at the beginning — the Earth's beginning, that is. Because we can't go back and see it all, we need to imagine our planet's transformation from a ball of hot gases to a planet of hot rock and molten lava and steam and volcanoes and earthquakes. Then we need to conjure up its slow change to a world of oceans and lakes, mountains and valleys, rivers and canyons, and, finally, plants and animals.

THE EARTH IS A LIVING CREATURE

Once we have imagined this transformation, we can begin to understand that our planet is not an unchanging ball of rock and dirt. We can begin to see that it is a living, ever-changing organism with a hot and molten heart, bones of rocks, muscles of earth, and blood of oil, water, and gas. We can begin to see it as a living creature with a varied skin of green trees and delicately scented flowers, of desert and seashore, of lakes and oceans, canyons and rivers. A creature which moves with grace and beauty through the vastness of space, wrapped in sunny skies and clouds, winds and rains. If we pay attention, we can feel that it is as alive and breathing and moving and changing as you and I.

At first it may be hard to think of the earth as a living organism, but it gets easier with practice, with learning what to look for, with realizing that all forms of life don't necessarily move as quickly as humans do. Nor do they lead the same kinds of lives. Take the Grand Canyon, for instance. Though its colorful walls may look lifeless at first glance, it is (of course) a part of this living creature, our earth. The many layers of rocks in the canyon's steep cliffs contain the past lives of millions of animals and plants — from tiny, one-celled creatures to trees hundreds of feet tall. Different kinds of rocks in the cliffs can even give us clues about what the weather was like during ancient times. If you look in the right places you can see the canyon move and change before your very eyes.

WHAT

THIS

BOOK

IS

ABOUT

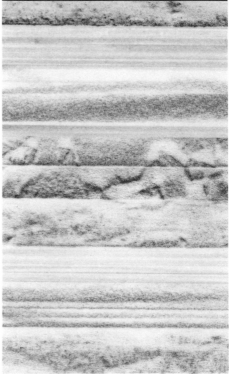

HIKING THROUGH HISTORY

In fact, the Grand Canyon is one of the few places on earth where we can see and touch, hike through and raft down such a large part of our planet's incredible life story. Here we can read of life on earth before the canyon began. We can see how layers of earth and rock were laid down by volcanoes and oceans, raised up as mountains, worn down by wind and sand and rain, walked on by ancient animals, imprinted by ancient plants — only to be layered and raised and worn down again and again. And each time this happened the layers of earth and rock and lava that were left behind preserved a bit of the earth's life in those long-ago times.

All these happenings are what you might call "ancient history" — they took place between two billion (2,000 million) and 200 million years ago. The story of how those layers of rock and bits of life have been unburied, so that we can read them today, you might call the Grand Canyon's "not-so-ancient history." The most "recent" part began when a river formed and began to cut a canyon (about six million years ago) and continued until the canyon became about as "grand" and as deep as it is today.

In this book we are first going to follow the course of the river we now call "Colorado" through rock, earth, and prehistory. We are going to watch it cut down through the bones of ancient animals and the leaves of ancient plants, through the layers of mountain tops and lake bottoms until it looks pretty much as it does today.

WHO FOUND THE GRAND CANYON?

This brings us to the time when another kind of history began in the Grand Canyon — human history. This is the story, first, of the early hunters and gatherers who came to North America and eventually to Grand Canyon country. These people built homes, and raised children and crops there for thousands of years before the Spanish explorers discovered the canyon in the 1500s. After the Spanish came other explorers, then scientists, naturalists, prospectors, artists, and other hardy travelers, such as the early tourists.

Each of these groups had its own way of looking at the Grand Canyon. Prospectors saw it as a place where they might make their fortunes in gold or other minerals. People emigrating west saw it as an inconvenient and dangerous obstacle in their journey across a mostly-unknown continent. Explorers sometimes saw it as a wonder of the world, like the pyramids of Egypt. Many adventurers looked at it as a challenge to their strength and ingenuity. And artists and scientists naturally looked at it as a fitting subject to paint, photograph, and study.

In 1903, when travel by road instead of by rail became possible, Teddy Roosevelt, the 26th American president, visited the Grand Canyon. He was so impressed with the canyon as a scenic, natural, and scientific wonder that he made it a National Monument. Several years later, in 1919, Grand Canyon National Monument became Grand Canyon National Park.

"G-R-A-N-D C-A-N-Y-O-N" SPELLS "ADVENTURE"!

After the Grand Canyon became a national park its human history took yet another direction. Trails and facilities were built to accommodate the many people who wanted to visit and explore the canyon — people like you and me. Today we can easily visit this natural scenic wonder, although "visit" is really much too tame a word.

Actually, nowadays you can have just about any kind of outdoor *adventure* you could wish for at the canyon (and even a few indoor ones). You can hike rim-to-rim, raft the Colorado, talk with ranger-naturalists, explore museums and Indian ruins, look for fossils, watch the sunrise from Yaki Point and the sunset from Desert View Watchtower, explore old roads, walk the South Rim from Hermits Rest to Yavapai Point and the North Rim from Grand Canyon Lodge to Point Imperial, picnic and camp in pine groves, and much more. You can even look on as deer graze, squirrels hide nuts, ravens ride the winds, and your fellow-visitors take photos.

WATCHING THE CANYON CHANGE

And while you are exploring the Grand Canyon in these ways, you can see for yourself that history is still being made here. You can watch the canyon growing and shrinking, crumbling and being built up. You can watch the Colorado River cutting the canyon deeper, moving boulders, changing its path. You can watch as lichens crumble the rocks and as wind and cold and water nibble down the rim. You can look on as deer graze, squirrels hide nuts, ravens ride the winds, and your fellow-visitors take photos. You can see and touch nature's records of ancient times.

YOU ARE A CANYON CREATURE

Not only that, but once you have been to the Canyon you will always be part of its ever-changing present and future, part of the community of living creatures which inhabit the Grand Canyon today. You will be just as much a part of it as the blue-striped lizards sunning on the rim rocks, the owls calling through the dusk, the tassel-eared squirrels scolding in the pine trees, and the gray fox stalking a rabbit. This is because it will have changed you and you will have changed it, just by your visit there. You will not forget the Canyon and it will not forget you.

WHY THE CANYON IS PART OF YOUR BACK YARD

The Grand Canyon is not just a collection of rocky views and petrified plants and animals, a place to buy hot dogs and ice cream and postcards, a place with weird squirrels and peculiar plants, or a place to try your muscles on steep, hot trails. It is a living, breathing, changing part of our planet. Like you, it is non-replaceable and needs protection from injury.

Even if you live several thousand miles away and only visit the Canyon once in your life, or even if you never visit it, it is still part of your own back yard. In fact, all of America's parks and wildernesses are part of your back yard. This is because these wild lands have been reserved for your use. These "reserved" wild places are "public lands." Public lands such as our National Parks and Monuments, our Wilderness Areas, our Wildlife Refuges, our State Parks, and even our city parks, are "owned" by you and all other Americans.

This means that the Grand Canyon's history, its present, and its future are important to each of us. And if we want to make sure that this part of our back yard will always be here to enjoy and learn from, we must treat it gently.

"Take only pictures and leave only footprints" is the best advice to follow whenever you visit a park or wilderness. (Squirrels actually have no good use for aluminum cans and gum wrappers. And the kids you may have someday would probably prefer to see those rim rocks in their original place rather than in a shoe box!)

So that's what this book is about—how the Canyon became "grand," the early people who lived there, the explorers who discovered it, the adventurers and scientists who first described it, the artists who painted and photographed it, the rafters who ran its river, the first tourists who visited it, the prospectors and what they found, how it became a national park, the animals and plants of yesterday and today, and the many ways you and your family can explore and get to know one of our planet's great natural wonders. See you there!

CHAPTER 1

HOW THE CANYON BECAME GRAND

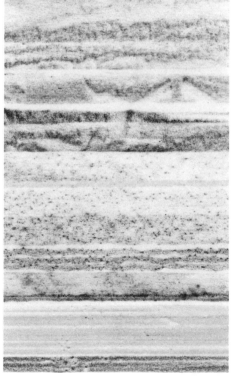

A BOOK OF ROCKS?

Many people, when they see the Grand Canyon for the first time, think it looks like an immense, beautifully colored crack in the earth. After looking at it for a while, though, people start to see a lot more than steep cliffs and bright colors.

For example, if visitors look for the Colorado River at the bottom of the Canyon, they may first see some rafts or boats. Then, they may catch sight of people riding mules on the trails below them. As they watch the mules they'll probably notice that the rock layers of the Canyon are in different colored strips — red, gray, tan, gold, brown, black, white. Some layers are thick and some are thin. Then the visitors may remember that the Colorado River cut the Canyon through the layers, and that those layers are like pages of a book. The book tells us what the earth was like before the Canyon, and about how the Canyon got to be so immense, so deep, and so brightly colored.

After looking at the Canyon's layers for a while, visitors may then begin talking to the rangers or looking through some books about the Grand Canyon to find out how it all began. They may begin to learn one of the earth's many languages, the language of the many-colored rock layers they see stretching from the Colorado River to both of the Canyon's rims.

A TRIP IN A TIME MACHINE

If you'd like to start learning this "earth language," you can try imagining for a few minutes that you have a chance to actually see how the Grand Canyon began. In fact, you've managed to get enough money together to rent a time machine for an hour. Time machine trips, as everyone knows, aren't cheap. Excited about your trip, you arrive at the terminal early and wait impatiently until it is your turn. Checking your watch, you step in through the gleaming door of the first vacant machine.

After looking over the instruction book quickly but carefully, you decide to begin at the beginning of earth's history in order to find out how all those rock layers got there in the first place. You waste no time, but seat yourself comfortably and immediately feed the proper number of coins into the slot.

In a friendly voice, the machine responds at once with, "Time Travelers, Inc., welcomes you. Please look at the screen. The numbers on the screen will indicate how many years before or after your time it is at the moment. 'M.y.a.' means 'millions of years ago' before your time. What times do you wish to visit?"

You check the display and note that your own time is showing on it, then explain that you'd like to find out how the Grand Canyon got to be the way it is. The machine instructs you to press the "begin" key.

Instantly, the glowing red figures on the display change to read "5 billion (5,000 million) years ago." Startled by the sudden change, you look quickly at the viewport and discover that you're now suspended far out in space above the earth.

5000 MILLION
YEARS AGO

START TIME
STOP

OFF

About 8 or 9 million years ago, parts of what is now the southwestern United States probably looked something like the illustration on pages 6 and 7. (This, of course, was several million years before the Colorado River began cutting the Grand Canyon.) At that time, herds of the first one-toed horses, the small *Pliohippus,* roamed the grass-covered plains. "Giraffe-camels" (*Alticamelus*) browsed among the smaller trees. Saber-toothed cats (*Machairodus*) lurked near waterholes, waiting for an unsuspecting animal to wander close enough to provide a meal. Shovel-tusked mastodons (*Platybelodon*) rooted in the mud for nourishing plants. *Teleoceras,* another vegetarian, was an amphibian which looked like a cross between a hippopotamus and a rhinoceros. Then there was the hardy mastodon of the time, *Mastodon americanus.* Unlike mastodons in other parts of the world, *americanus* was hairy! This creature reached a length of 12 feet and was so tough that it survived in North America until a few thousand years ago.

The Earth Shapes Up

As you catch your breath and look down, you first see a swirling ball of clouds. But not for long. The numbers on the display begin to flicker faster and faster, showing that you are racing toward the present. Soon the clouds begin to break up. You see vast seas, then great bodies of land rising from the oceans, moving about, bumping into each other like leaves in a puddle on a windy day. You see continents changing shape, coming together to form huge land masses, and moving apart or breaking up into smaller pieces.

In order to get a better view of this activity, you ask the machine to take you closer to the earth's surface in the region where the Grand Canyon will someday be.

As you hover thousands of feet up you see mountain ranges pushing up out of the earth, then being worn down by wind and rain into boulders and, finally, into sand and dirt. At the same time, great cracks open in the ground and new mountains push up again and again.

The land rises and falls; water sometimes covers it from horizon to horizon. Lakes fill and rivers form — then disappear, leaving behind huge basins and long valleys of mud. Volcanoes throw up ash and ooze lava from deep inside the earth. While you're still trying to make sense of this startling spectacle, the machine asks if you'd like to know a little about what's going on underneath the earth's surface and causing all this activity.

"Yeah, but how do I stop this thing?" you say, knowing that it'll be impossible to concentrate with so much going on outside.

"Just press the 'time stop' button to your right," the machine replies.

Feeling a little foolish, you press the button. Outside the viewport, the world seems to have come to a sudden stop. Thousands of feet below you is a flat mass of greenery dotted with lakes and surrounded by mountains. To the south, over the mountains, there is a layer of something dark, maybe smoke or ash from volcanic eruptions. The display reads "65 m.y.a."

"Where are all the mountains and volcanoes?" you ask, now used to talking to the machine that surrounds you.

"I think, if you'll pardon the word," says the machine, "that it'll be easier to explain things if we aren't right on top of them."

"Fine with me," you say. "Go ahead."

"Right. Well, the latest theories in your time go something like this: The earth hasn't always been as solid as it is in your time. And even in your time — the 21st century, that is — it isn't as solid as many people think it is. By the way, watch the screen to your left and I'll show you what probably happened as I go along.

"Anyway, many billions of years ago the earth and the other planets in the solar system were probably hot, gaseous balls, like the top screen shows. But as the gases cooled and their molecules got closer together, some of the balls became more solid, like the bottom screen. By about 4.6 billion years ago, a rigid crust several miles thick had formed over the earth, but the part under the crust stayed hot and soft.

225 million years ago　　　　　**160 million years ago**

"The part under the crust was and is pretty dense, but because it isn't solid it has currents in it. These currents deep inside the earth push against the rigid crust, which has cracked over time to form several pieces called 'plates.' As the currents deep in the earth push against the plates, they move. The continents which sit on the plates move, too. So, as you can see, the earth hasn't always looked like it does in your time. And the part that's now the Grand Canyon hasn't always been in the same place.

"But that's just the big picture. On a smaller scale, for example in the region where the Grand Canyon eventually is carved out by the Colorado River, all the plate pushing has some pretty interesting effects. One thing that happens as the plates of the earth's crust are pushed together is that wrinkles are formed. These wrinkles are mountain ranges. When the plates are pulled apart, mountains may disappear and valleys take their place. And whenever the plates move, there are earthquakes.

"During the early part of the earth's history, when its interior was hotter and the plates moved around more, there were a lot more volcanoes than there are in your time. Volcanoes form when earthquakes open up holes or fissures in the crust that allow hot gases and liquid rock to be pushed up to the surface from the earth's hot interior. There has always been a lot of volcanic activity in the area where the Grand Canyon formed because it's near the edge of one of the plates."

"That's enough for now, thanks," you say quickly as the machine pauses while searching for more information. "How about

65 million years ago   **Present Time**

going forward and seeing what things looked like before the canyon started to form?"

Arrival in No-Canyon Time

"Your request is Time Travelers, Inc.'s command," the machine quickly responds.

Once more the display begins to flicker. Looking down on the region where the Grand Canyon will be in the future, you see a flat area circled with mountains. Pretty soon the flat part seems to bulge slowly upward. Then you see that the high mountains around the plateau seem to be drifting further apart and crumbling as hundreds of centuries of wind and rain wear away layers of dirt and rock and lava. Soon, some parts of the plateau are sticking up above the rest.

The animated reference screen now shows that this is where the Grand Canyon will begin forming. Once more, you reach for the "time stop" key. When the display stops flickering, it reads "10 m.y.a."

When you get down to only a few hundred feet above the ground, the machine opens the ventilation system to the fresh outside air.

The air is warm, and the plateau is lush with grass, flowers, and trees. You're close enough to see that many animals are moving slowly through the grassland, but you're too far away to tell what kinds they are — although one looks a lot like a camel. You wonder what it would be like to go down and explore a little.

A

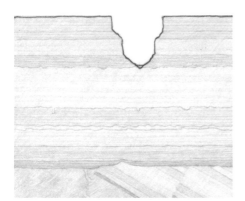

B

(A) A creek or small river begins to erode the layers of the Kaibab Plateau about 5 million years ago.

(B) Time passes. The small river is joined by other creeks and becomes larger as the Kaibab Plateau is pushed up higher. The steeper slope makes it easier for the water to cut through more layers.

The machine senses your thought and quickly says, "I'm sorry, but you can't walk around among the life forms in another time zone. Time Travelers, Inc., can take no chances on customers changing the course of history by accidentally stepping on an ancestor. Please accept our apologies for not being able to offer you a complete experience. Now, I think we'd better move on and see how the Colorado cut the Grand Canyon before your time (if you'll pardon the word) runs out."

Only slightly disappointed (after all, some of the animals look rather large), you ask, "If I can't go down there, how about filling me in on how the Colorado River made the Grand Canyon look the way it does in my time?"

"No problem with that," replies the machine. "How about taking us up the Colorado to about the place where Grand Canyon Village overlooks the river in your time?"

"Sure," you say, happy to have a chance to fly the capsule again yourself. Taking the manual controls, you glance one last time at the peaceful plain outside the view port, then check the display, which still reads 10 m.y.a. Pressing the "slow speed" and "forward" keys, you ease the stick down and to your right until you are skimming east along the canyon several thousand feet above the river.

When the bright dot on the animated map reaches the "future Grand Canyon Village" marker, you press the "stop" key.

Below you, in a narrow gorge, the Colorado River is flowing west across the Kaibab Plateau.

The Canyon Grows Grander

"If we go forward in time at 40,000 years per second," the machine says, "it will take about two minutes to see how the canyon becomes grand. Do you want to start now?"

"In a minute. First tell me something about what's going to be happening and why, so it'll make more sense," you say.

"Good idea," replies the machine. "Here, take a look at the viewscreen to your left. That's a cross-section of the canyon. The little "V" at the top is probably what the river's channel looks like from the time we're in now — which is five-and-one-half million years before your time. The big, scooped-out "U" on the outside with the little "v" at the bottom is what the river's canyon looks like in your time. The outlines in between show how the river has changed from small channel to huge canyon."

"The way rivers get started and canyons get carved goes something like this. First you have some sloping land, like the Kaibab Plateau. There also has to be water — lots of it. It helps if there are some mountains nearby to catch rain and snow from storms and cause it to run across the sloping land.

"If the land is flat or saucer-like instead of sloping, the water from rain and snow forms lakes or marshes. But when the land slopes, the water runs across it, forming little waterfalls over rocks and digging out the softer dirt parts. When the water digs even a small channel, it starts to move dirt, then pebbles and small rocks. As rocks are pushed along by water, they scrape away more dirt and more rocks.

"Meanwhile, as water in the channel flows downhill, it's also eating away at the place where the channel begins. (This eating away is called "erosion.") So, the water is eroding away the rocks and dirt at its highest point. This is the main way streams get longer.

"Sometimes the land the stream is flowing over gets pushed up higher. (Remember the plates bumping against each other?) When this happens, water cuts into the ground even faster. After a while, depending on how steep the slope is, and how much water flows down the channel and how often, the stream may get long enough, wide enough, or deep enough to be called a river.

Oceans and Layers

"Very few rivers carve spectacular canyons, though. The conditions have to be just right for that to happen. You've already seen part of what happened that will later make the Colorado River's canyon so spectacular. Do you remember?"

"I think so," you respond. "It happened awfully fast, but about two billion years ago the whole area where the Grand Canyon is in

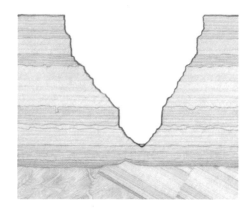

C

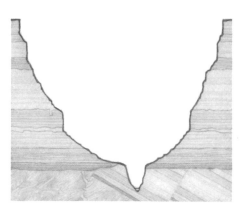

D

(C) As the plateau continues to push up, and layers wear away, the Grand Canyon begins to take shape. By about 4 million years ago, the Canyon is almost as deep as it is in our time.

(D) By about 1 million years ago, the Grand Canyon looks much like it does today.

A

B

C

(A) The oldest rocks in the Grand Canyon, the Vishnu schists and granites, were mountains about 1700 million years ago. Today, these dark rocks are at the bottom of the Colorado River gorge.

(B) These ancient mountains were then worn down almost flat by erosion. As hundreds of millions of years went by, many layers were deposited on top by huge seas which came and went.

(C) During these hundreds of millions of years, the layers were pushed up into mountains several times. Each time the mountains were worn away, another sea would again deposit more sediments.

my time was covered by water — an ocean, I guess. The floor of the ocean was sagging and layers of sand and dirt and volcanic rocks and other sediments were making layers there. Then I saw mountains pushed up out of the ocean and worn down almost flat by water and wind, right?

"Then an ocean came in again — I'm not sure when — and then some more mountains were pushed up and eroded down. Then there may have been more oceans and mountains, but I don't quite remember.

"Finally, at about 600 million years before my time, there was another ocean. This ocean kept going in and out, making more layers, for over 500 million years. When that ocean pulled away — it hasn't come back yet — what was left behind looked like a big saucer with mountains all around it.

"But pretty soon the floor of the saucer got pushed up so that it was only a little lower than the mountains. Then, about 20 million years before my time, the mountains got pulled apart and things started to look about like they do now, down below. The layers of sediments from the oceans and the dirt and sand layers from mountain erosion got all covered up by other layers, but when the river cuts down through them and makes the canyon — "

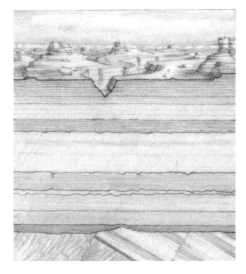

D   **E**

The machine interrupts you with, "Not bad, not bad. You seem to have learned a lot on our little trip. Before we start going forward in time again and watching the Colorado dig out the Grand Canyon, you may be wondering what happened to the animals and plants that were around while all the layer-making was going on."

Plants, Animals, and Fossils

"Animals and plants? Oh, sure. I saw a lot of those. What did happen to them?"

"They didn't just disappear, of course," the machine says. "A lot of them are still down there in the layers. Sometimes, when animals and plants die, their bodies, or maybe even just their footprints, get covered up by water or dirt or rocks. Then they may be turned to stone by minerals and water. Finally, you have fossils.

"The area around Grand Canyon probably has more rock layers and fossils right out there where people can see them than any place else on Earth. All those layers are what make the Grand Canyon interesting and important, as well as spectacular. Everyone from the explorers and prospectors of the late 1800s to the artists and scientists of the 1900s to the hikers and other sightseers of your time seems to agree about that. Now, shall we —"

(D) By about 5 million years ago, the region where the Grand Canyon was going to form looked about like it does today — except that there wasn't any Canyon yet.

(E) It only took another few million years for the Kaibab Plateau to push up further and for a creek to become the Colorado River, cutting the Grand Canyon we know today.

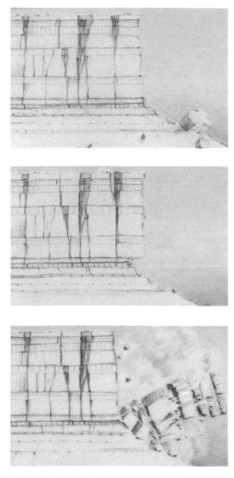

As a river cuts a canyon, it leaves cliffs behind. Wind and water, heat and cold, all help wear away the softer materials in a cliff, causing pieces of the canyon walls to fall off. This is why the Grand Canyon keeps getting wider and wider.

But before the machine can finish its sentence, bright blue warning lights start flashing and all the viewscreens change to read, "TIME RETURN COUNTDOWN: 120 seconds . . . 119 seconds . . ."

"O.K., O.K.," you say, taking a deep breath while keying in "40,000 years per second" and then pressing the "enter" key. "Here we go!"

The capsule instantly plunges forward and down as if it's gone over a waterfall, and you grab for the joystick in a hurry. "Sorry," you mumble, "must have been leaning on that by accident."

"Never mind," the machine says, "crashes aren't in my program. Just look out the viewport and tell me what you see."

Wind, Water, and Rock

"Hey, it's a good thing I did get us down closer, even if it was sort of an accident," you say when you see what's happening just outside. "We're so close, you can see how water breaks off little pieces of rock and how ice kind of pries some pretty big pieces of rock right off the canyon walls. And the river's already cut down into the plateau quite a ways. Looks like some of the layers are a lot softer than others, too. The soft layers fall apart or get worn away faster than the hard layers. The hard layers are mostly making cliffs. But why are a lot of the rock layers turning reddish? Aren't they light-colored at first when a big piece falls off?"

"Whatever color a rock is on the surface has to do with the minerals in it. There's a lot of iron in some of the Canyon's pink, red, and yellow rocks," replies the machine.

"Hey, isn't the canyon getting wider now?" you ask, pulling back on the stick and easing the capsule up a side canyon.

"That's right. Can you see why?" the machine asks.

"Well, it looks to me like water from storms on the plateau starts making waterfalls over the canyon's edge. The waterfalls chew away at the edge until they make side canyons. Lots of side canyons. Sometimes the side canyons are close enough together that they meet. This leaves little plateaus, like islands, in the canyon. There's one forming right now," you say, steering the

capsule back into the main canyon. "And it's not staying a plateau. It's getting pointy."

"Like this?" the machine asks, lighting up a screen.

"Uh-huh. The pictures I've seen of the Grand Canyon show lots of those, and they all have strange names, like 'Zoroaster Temple' and 'Vishnu Temple.' But I can see they don't stay that way. Look, that one's gone already!" you say, feeling like your time is rapidly running out.

Last Stop at Today

A glance at the display tells you that the 21st century is only seconds away. Out the viewport, the Grand Canyon grows deeper and wider until it looks just like all the pictures you've seen. You can tell that sometime in the future it will no longer be an incredibly beautiful canyon, but a vast, flat, river valley. "Can't we stop for just one more close look?" you ask.

"I'm afraid there isn't time," the machine replies.

"But there are lots of things I really want to see now that I've got it all scoped out!"

"Well, I guess you'll have to see them all in your own time," the machine says soothingly, as the viewport closes with a soft click. "Time Travelers, Inc. doesn't allow anyone to visit the same place more than once, you know."

Feeling a little weird, you slowly let go of the joystick, press the seat's safety system "off" key, and stand up. For a moment, what you've seen of the Grand Canyon and the Colorado River seems more real to you than anything in your own time. But then, as you begin to feel a little less weird, you remember that the Canyon is part of your time. And that, in fact, you and your family are going to Grand Canyon National Park soon. That's why you took this trip in the first place.

Not quite sure whether you're expected to thank a machine, you mutter, "Uh, it was great. Thanks a lot."

"Time Travelers, Inc. is glad you are satisfied with your trip. We try to provide the best experience possible. Don't forget to pick up your souvenir book on the way out. You'll find it contains interesting information on the subject of your trip," the machine says in its most polite voice.

With a soft swoosh the capsule's door opens. You can see the next customer shifting from one foot to the other behind the entrance gate outside the capsule. You pick up your book from the Auto-Vend slot and step quickly outside into the busy terminal, hearing a rather un-machinelike "Happy exploring!"

As you glance back, surprised, the next customer is stepping eagerly into the capsule. You hear "Time Travelers, Inc. welcomes — ," then the capsule's door closes with a click. Taking a deep breath, you turn and begin to walk quickly toward the people-mover. While stuffing the souvenir book into your jacket pocket, you notice the title: *Exploring the Grand Canyon — Adventures of Yesterday & Today*.

"All right!" you say to yourself.

CHAPTER 2

THE FIRST CANYON PEOPLE

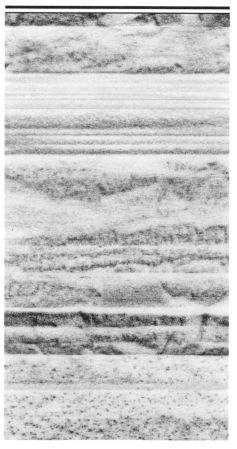

On a warm day in late
summer, an Anasazi village in
the Grand Canyon area may
have looked like the one
pictured on the preceding
pages. Notice the rabbit sticks
in the hands of the hunters, the
person hanging corn to dry, the
women grinding corn and
shaping pottery, and the
children playing games.

*Split-twig figures are made of willow
(top) or grass (bottom).*

THE MYSTERY OF THE STICK FIGURES

Have you ever crossed your fingers, knocked on wood, rubbed a rabbit's foot or looked for a four-leafed clover for good luck? If so, you probably have something in common with the early people who traveled through the Grand Canyon area thousands of years ago and left behind hundreds of mysterious stick figures. These "good luck" figures are made of single willow twigs which have been split, bent, and twisted into the shapes of deer, antelope, mountain sheep, and other animals the people hunted. All stick figures have been found in limestone caves high on the canyon walls, so some of these long-ago travelers must have been excellent rock climbers.

Some of the animal figures have a small spear or cactus thorn thrust through them, as if the hunters were trying to magically ensure they would be able to do the same to a real animal. Some figures were found in shrine-like arrangements of stones and included what might have been prayer-sticks, with feathers and human hair attached. All the stick figures seem to have been carefully placed. Because of this evidence, today's experts on ancient Southwestern peoples feel that the animal figures were made and put in the caves to bring good luck to hunters.

But where did these makers of stick figures come from? Well, to answer even part of that question, prehistorians have to go a long way back in time and a long way from the Southwest. How far back? Well, we need to go back at least 12,000 years, to the time when early people began crossing into North America from Siberia on a land bridge. This "bridge" is still there, of course, but it's now under water! People were able to travel across the bridge during the Ice Ages when mile-thick sheets of ice were using up a lot of the Pacific Ocean's water. When this happened, the water level of the ocean became much lower and parts of the ocean's "floor" were exposed. Today the Bering Strait is a wide sea channel separating Siberia and Alaska.

Many of the hardy people who walked across the land bridge didn't just stop when they got to the other side, of course. The

About 12,000 years ago, when there was a land bridge between what are now Russia and Alaska, people were able to migrate into North America. Although vast ice sheets covered much of northern Canada at this time, for a while there was a "corridor" through the ice which allowed people to get through to the more southerly, ice-free parts of the continent. When the corridor closed, people who had to remain in the far north became the Native Americans we know as Eskimos. By about 10,000 years ago, descendents of people who had passed through the corridor had reached South America.

ones who did settle in what we now call Alaska are known today as Eskimos. The people who kept exploring southward eventually spread into what became Canada, the U.S., Mexico, and South America. Today, we call these people "Native Americans."

So, we know that the ancestors of the people who left the stick figures in caves high in the walls of Grand Canyon originally had come across the land bridge many thousands of years before. But there are still plenty of mysteries. For example, we still don't know where in North America these people had come from most recently, what they were like, how many of them there were, or exactly why they left the figures in the canyon.

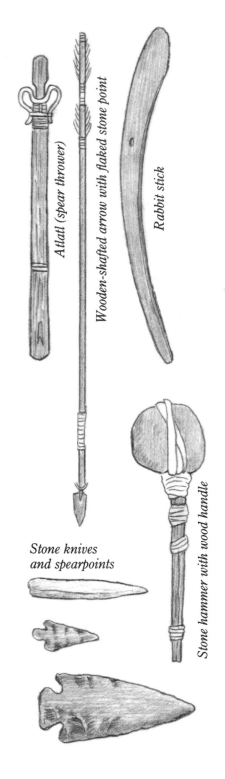

Atlatl (spear thrower)

Wooden-shafted arrow with flaked stone point

Rabbit stick

Stone hammer with wood handle

Stone knives and spearpoints

Prehistorians believe that the people who left the stick figures probably lived in or around the canyon, at least during part of the year. Others might have come from greater distances during the seasons when hunting was good and plant foods were easy to find. They, too, may have fashioned "good luck charms." From the time these stick figures were left high in the canyon walls (about 4000 years ago) to the time 1500 years ago when the Anasazi arrived, there are no other signs of humans at the Grand Canyon. ("Anasazi," by the way, means "ancient ones." This name was given to them only a few hundred years ago by the Navajos, when they moved into the areas where the Anasazi had once lived.)

WHO WERE THE ANASAZI?

To answer this question, we need to look back at the groups of people who came across the Bering Land Bridge and began moving south, looking for better places to live. Thousands of years later, they reached what is now the southwestern United States.

After they had been in the Southwest for a few thousand years, these people began to show some signs of settling down for at least part of the year. Instead of using only "sleeping circles" with low stone walls and no roof, they began building more sturdy and permanent shelters. Their huts also became more elaborate, as they began putting up walls and roofs of brush and mud that were supported by posts. They also built storage rooms for excess food and cooking pits lined with rocks.

Other changes had to do with tools. For thousands of years these people had been chipping knives and spearpoints for hunting and stone tools for chopping, scraping, and grinding seeds, nuts, and roots. As they expanded their skills, they began to carve spear-throwing sticks called "atlatls" (AT-lat-uhls), work bone, weave baskets and sandals, and make traps for catching birds and small animals such as squirrels and rabbits.

As time went on, these people had so successfully adapted themselves to living in the semi-desert lands of the Southwest that there were hundreds of little groups of them.

Now that they were living a somewhat more settled life than they once did, these people began learning the skills which would eventually turn them from hunters of plant foods and small animals into farmers. Their "teachers" were other groups of people traveling into the Southwest. The groups exchanged both skills and goods. From the south (Mexico) came the first seeds of corn, squash, and (later) beans.

More time passed. More skills were exchanged. The people became very handy at making bows and arrows for hunting, shell jewelry, various kinds of carrying and cooking baskets, and decorated pottery.

As the years went by, they began to meet the groups from the south more often. These groups, who had earlier carried seeds to the Southwest, now brought knowledge of ways to water crops. As a result, many of the people in the Southwest had become part-time villagers. Although they still used many wild foods, they also grew corn, squash, and beans.

As time passed, these people spread throughout the mountain, desert, and plateau areas of the Southwest. The "Anasazi" were groups who lived on the Colorado plateau. As mentioned before, this name now means "ancient ones."

So that's who the Anasazi were. They're not quite as mysterious as the leavers of the stick figures, because — as you'll soon see — they left much more behind for us to learn from. Remember, then, as we talk about the Anasazi who settled in the Grand Canyon area, that they haven't just appeared out of nowhere. They were the descendants of people who had already lived in the Southwest for thousands of years — who were the descendants of the people who came across the Bering Land Bridge, who were . . . Well, you get the idea.

THE CANYON'S FIRST SETTLERS

It was over a thousand years ago when groups of the Anasazi people began living around and in the Grand Canyon. By this time, they were experts at making beautiful baskets of yucca leaves and

Early pottery and baskets.

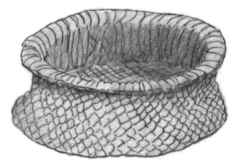

These Anasazi ruins are under a cliff on the Canyon's North Rim.

grass which they used for carrying loads and for storing food. For this reason, prehistorians sometimes call these Anasazi "Basket-makers."

But the Anasazi of this time did more than just make baskets. They had also learned how to finger-weave intricate sandals and bags, as well as men's loincloths and women's tiny "apron-skirts." For keeping warm in cold weather, they interlaced rabbit fur or deerskin strips to make capes and blankets. They also tamed wild turkeys and kept them in their villages like people today keep chickens.

The Anasazi also made several kinds and colors of pottery, which they decorated with many different designs. Because pottery can be used in so many ways, it began to take the place of some of the earlier intricate baskets. They made pottery bowls, ladles, jars, pitchers, and even canteens.

Although the Anasazi were still gathering many wild foods at this time, they had become skilled at growing corn, beans, and squash. They no longer just poked a few seeds in the ground and then depended on nature do the rest. Instead, they developed methods of using the Colorado Plateau's occasional rains. One method was to guide rainwater from higher areas to the crops by piling up lines of rocks or digging shallow ditches.

By the time the Anasazi came to the Grand Canyon, some groups were building box-like rooms of stones put together with mud—like people today build with bricks and mortar. These rooms were usually attached to each other and built in a row or an "L" or "U" shape.

A couple of hundred years later, some Anasazi buildings were several stories high. Today, we call this type of a building a "pueblo," and prehistorians sometimes call these Anasazi "Pueblo Indians." ("Pueblo" is a Spanish word meaning "village." The Spanish explorers of the 1500s were the first to call the native people of the Southwest "Pueblo Indians.")

When the Anasazi pueblo builders first began settling here and there around the Grand Canyon, some settled on the south side of the canyon and others settled on the north. A few groups even tried living at the bottom of the canyon. Within a few hundred years there were Anasazi villages on both rims and at the bottom of the canyon, by the Colorado River. And in just a few hundred years more, the Anasazi were gone again. They moved out of the Grand Canyon area looking for better places to live. Fortunately for us, though, they left some pretty interesting things behind.

Ever since the early part of this century, people have been carefully looking at what the Anasazi left behind. Because the Anasazi had no written language, there is a lot we'll never know about them. For example, we'll never know the details of their religious life, music, games, and stories. Luckily, there are still plenty of things we can know. We know what they wore, what they cooked with, how they made their clothing and cooking utensils, and what they made them of. We know what they ate and how old they lived to be. We know which foods they hunted and which they raised as crops. We know where they lived and for how long. We know how they built their homes and what materials they used. And a lot more.

VISIT TO AN ANCIENT VILLAGE

Most of the places where the Anasazi once lived aren't easy for today's Grand Canyon visitors to get to. A great many of them are far from any road or trail. The remains of some settlements are on top of plateaus that were once part of the Canyon's rims but which are now "islands." (The Powell Plateau is an example of this kind of "island." Today's canyon visitors can see the Powell Plateau from Pima or Hopi Point.) Other settlements were even built under some of the north rim's overhanging cliffs. Still others were built near the river at the bottom of the Canyon. Many of them are still being studied.

Even if you could visit the ruins of these old settlements today, you'd probably have a hard time figuring out what life was like for the people who once lived there. Luckily for us, prehistorians have been hard at work doing just that kind of figuring ever since the early part of this century. Tusayan (TU-suh-yahn), on the Grand

The ruins of Tusayan show that the pueblo was "U"-shaped. The round structures were kivas.

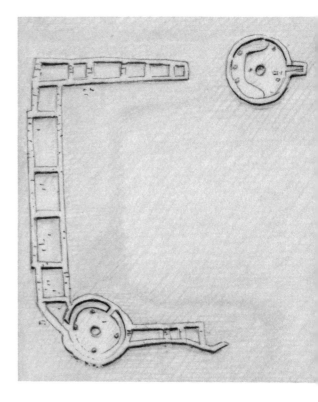

The interior of a kiva at Tusayan may have looked like this.

Canyon's south rim, is one of the Anasazi villages prehistorians now know a lot about.

But Tusayan pueblo is different than most Anasazi villages around the Grand Canyon in that it's not far away down a rough trail, under a cliff, or at the bottom of a canyon. Instead, Tusayan and its museum are only a few miles east of Grand Canyon Village, and have a good road going right to them. As you might guess, Tusayan is one of Grand Canyon National Park's most-visited places.

What Tusayan Looked Like

Because Tusayan has been so carefully excavated, people who visit there get a good idea of what life in an Anasazi village was probably like. If you were there at Tusayan right now, you'd be able to see that the pueblo was built in the shape of a square "U." The bottom of the "U" was a high row of rooms where people cooked, ate, and slept. The two sides of the "U" were rows of rooms used for storing food and other necessary items. The center of the "U" was open.

This open "plaza" was where people did just about everything as long as the weather was warm enough. If you could go back in time and stroll unseen around the Tusayan plaza, you'd probably see people weaving intricate baskets, carefully smoothing or painting pottery, grinding dry kernels of corn with stone "metate" and "mano," and perhaps building a new storage room. Almost everyone except the tiniest children would be doing some kind of daily task.

Close by the plaza, but not part of living and storage areas, was a round, sunken structure called a "kiva," which was used partly as a gathering place for the men of the village and partly as the village ceremonial center. People entered the kiva through an opening in the roof and climbed down a ladder to the bench-lined floor. The kiva and all the pueblo's buildings were made of flat limestone rocks put together with mortar made from mud mixed with dried twigs. Tree trunks were used for roof beams. Brush was laid over the beams and plastered with more mortar.

Today, the tree trunks used for roof beams can tell the pueblo's age. This is done by taking a very small sample of the beam's growth rings. The rings are wider in wetter years and narrower when the years are dry. The pattern of growth rings over time is something like a fingerprint because the pattern is unique. Rings can be used to tell how old a tree is and also something about an area's weather. By taking samples of the tree trunks used as roof beams at Tusayan, experts at tree-ring dating have figured out that the pueblo must have been built about 800 years ago. They also discovered that the weather was pretty dry about the time when people moved away from Tusayan.

Tusayan pueblo may have looked like this when the Anasazi were living there in the late 1100s.

The People of Tusayan

No one knows *exactly* what the Anasazi who lived at Tusayan looked like, but we do know they were shorter than most of us today. They seem to have made and worn simple clothes of cotton — loincloths for the men and apron-skirts for the women — and to have woven yucca sandals. Children probably wore little or nothing, at least during warm weather. In cold weather everyone probably wore capes and blankets made with furry animal skins.

And, just like people of today, the Tusayan villagers had to spend a lot of their time making sure they had enough to eat. They hunted deer, antelope, and bighorn sheep with bows and arrows as well as spears thrown with the help of the atlatl. Older children may have stalked and killed rabbits and squirrels with clubs or trapped them with nets or snares made of grass twine. At some times of the year, almost everyone in the pueblo may have collected wild foods such as pinyon nuts, yucca pods, and cactus fruits.

Each year, too, the people of Tusayan planted the corn, beans, and squash that made up about half their diet. To guide water to their crops, they piled rocks in long, low rows to catch rain and water from melting snow. When they had a good year, they dried and stored their surplus crops.

Although the Tusayan pueblo people had to work hard for their food and shelter, they still had plenty of time for fun and relaxing. Many of the things they left behind when they eventually moved to other pueblos to the east of the Grand Canyon show that they enjoyed wearing jewelry and playing games.

Some of the games played at Tusayan were probably much like the games played by pueblo peoples in the last century. Racing, for example, was one of the most popular outdoor games. Besides just racing for fun (in relays or by kicking sticks around a long course), some races were run to keep the sun going across the sky or to start streams racing down the gullies in spring. Then there were throwing games. One of these was sort of like horseshoes. A stone or corncob was stuck into the ground and the players threw flat stones at it, trying to knock it down. Small children played with

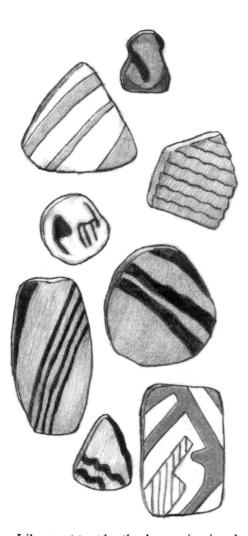

Like most people, the Anasazi enjoyed playing games. They made game pieces out of bone, shell, and clay. Some, like the ones shown here, may have started out as pieces of broken pottery. Unfortunately, the early Southwestern peoples had no written language, so no one knows exactly how their games were played. (Poker chips and dice are examples of game pieces we use today.)

carved dolls and spun tops by hand (they kept them going with a stick, instead of using string). There were also bow-and-arrow games, dart games, singing games, guessing games, and even gambling games. In their gambling games, the pueblo people used "dice" which were quite different than the kind we use. Instead of cubes (which are hard to carve) they used bits of bone or short sticks, painted in different ways. Some of these games were very complicated and took a lot of skill. And it wasn't just the kids who played games — just like today, people of all ages enjoyed them!

Another thing almost everyone at the pueblo enjoyed was wearing jewelry and nice clothes. But the raw materials for little luxuries like shell and turquoise jewelry or cotton for weaving clothes weren't found near Tusayan. The people of the pueblo probably traded their pottery and finely-made baskets with other villagers for them. Shell and turquoise, however, probably came from villages as far as 100 miles away. In turn, those far-away villages traded with people a long distance from them. Cotton, for example, came primarily from South America. So, in the course of time and many trades, turquoise from western Arizona and shells from the Pacific Coast or the Gulf of California reached Tusayan. Here, the cotton was woven into loincloths and the shell and turquoise made into necklaces, bracelets, and hair ornaments. In other words, these people were much like us, even though they lived much more simply.

Surprisingly, the villagers left Tusayan about 30 years or so after building it. In trying to figure out why they left so soon, prehistorians have looked at samples of tree rings from that time. The narrow rings show that the climate was getting drier and drier on the Canyon's south rim. It may be that the villagers' crops got smaller and smaller, until there wasn't enough food to feed everyone. Hunger may have forced the Anasazi to leave Tusayan for places to the east of Grand Canyon where there was more water for their crops. The Hopi (HO-pee) people, who live today in villages to the east of the Canyon, are descendents of the "ancient ones." Some of their ancestors may even have come from Tusayan.

"YOU ARE WELCOME
TO COME UP HERE . . ."

There are also some interesting tales of how the Grand Canyon was formed. Some relatives of the Havasupais, the Walapais, say that in very ancient times a monstrous flood covered the earth with water. All the living creatures were drowned or trapped by the flood except for Pack-i-tha-wi. He waded into the water carrying a big flint knife and a heavy wooden club. He used the club to pound the knife into the earth under the water. As he pounded and moved the knife back and forth he made the Grand Canyon. When it was big enough and long enough, the water all rushed out into the Sea of the Sunset. Then the sun came out and baked the land until it was dry and cracked like it is today.

As you know, the geologists of our time have different ideas and explanations for how the Grand Canyon came to be. But there are many ways of seeing the world, and interesting stories like these, and the Hopi story below, are among them.

To the Hopis, the Grand Canyon is a very special place — the place where their ancestors first emerged from the underworld through a hole in the ground called the "sipapu." Here is one tale of their coming-into-the-world.

At one time the people were living underground all crowded together. They wanted to escape, so they sent a bird, Motsni, up to the surface to see if anyone was there who would welcome them. Motsni flew out through Sipapu and looked around. At first the bird saw no one. After flying around for a while, Motsni finally saw somebody sitting on the ground.

The somebody said, "Sit down, you flying around there, sit down. Certainly you are flying around for some reason."

"Well, yes," Motsni replied, and he told the figure that the people underground wanted to know if there was anyone in the upper world who would welcome them.

"You may call me Masau'u," the figure said. "As you can see, this is the way I am living here. I am living in poverty. I have nothing. This is the way I am living here. If the people are willing to live here like this with me until they die, they are welcome."

Motsni flew back into the underworld.

The people asked the bird, "What did you find out?"

"I found Masau'u," Motsni said. "He lives there poorly, he doesn't have much. But if you want to live that way, too, you are welcome to come up there."

"All right," the people said. "So that is the way he is saying. We are welcome, and we are going."

When the people had all gone through Sipapu and arrived in the upper world, they met Masau'u.

"Will you give us permission to live here?" they asked.

"Yes," Masau'u said. "But first there are some things you need to know about your place in the world. It is to the north from here and its color is yellowish white. The chiefs of your land are the juniper tree, the owl, the mountain lion, and others you will learn of later. You have not yet come to the place where you will settle down. You must follow your stars to that place. Go to the north and claim your land." Then he disappeared.

The people all looked at one another. Then they started to travel in the direction Masau'u had showed them.

CHAPTER 3

EARLY CANYON ADVENTURERS

As you can see from the illustration on the preceding pages, the Powell expedition found running the rapids of the "Grand River" (the Colorado) in the "Big Canyon" (the Grand Canyon) both dangerous and exciting!

After the Anasazi left the country around the Grand Canyon to move east, about 800 years ago, other groups of Native Americans in the area continued to live their simple lives for several hundred years. Then, about 500 years ago, in the early 1500s, Spanish soldier- adventurers (called "Conquistadores" — "the conquerors") took over the lands we now call Mexico. They called this area "New Spain." Not satisfied with the golden wealth of the Aztecs in "New Spain," the Spaniards sent expeditions north to look for more lands to conquer. One expedition "discovered" the Grand Canyon.

SOLDIERS AND MISSIONARIES

The first foreigners to see the Grand Canyon in August of 1540 probably wished they hadn't. This unlucky party of thirteen Spanish soldiers, led by Garcia Lopez de Cardenas, had been sent by the explorer Francisco Vasquez de Coronado to find a great river rumored to reach from the Gulf of California far into the interior of the New World . . . a river that might help the Spanish find the fabled "golden" cities of Cibola.

The horseman in the heavy armor (center) is Francisco Vasquez de Coronado, a Spanish soldier who, in 1540, led the first big European expedition into what is now the American Southwest. A group of Coronado's men, commanded by Garcia Lopez de Cardenas, became the first Europeans to see the Grand Canyon.

Well, Cardenas found the river, all right. He and his men and horses marched hard and long through heavy pine forests and rugged canyons, with little food and less water, to reach it. And when they did reach it (probably somewhere near today's Desert View, about 25 miles east of Grand Canyon Village), the river was several thousand feet below them at the bottom of a vast, steep-sided canyon. They were not impressed. Spanish explorers of the 1500s were looking for easy routes to riches and to lands they could claim for their king. They were not looking for scenic beauty. And they were certainly not looking for canyons that were impossible to cross. But that's what they found.

The exhausted and disappointed travelers spent several days riding their scrawny horses along the canyon rim, looking for a way down to the chocolate-colored river at the bottom of the abyss. They didn't find one. (Their Hopi guides knew of several, but they weren't talking.) Three of the soldiers even tried to climb down the steep cliffs to the river. They gave up when rocks that looked the size of a man from the rim turned out to be several hundred feet high. From a few hundred feet down the cliffs the men also saw that the river was much wider than the six feet Cardenas had thought. Which was what the Hopis had been telling them all along.

So, Cardenas and his men, short on supplies and probably short of temper, made their hungry way back to their commander. Coronado, too, was not impressed. He wanted news of a good way to reach the fabled cities said to contain gold and emeralds, or at least turquoise. He wasn't the least interested in tales of an unreachable river at the bottom of an uncrossable canyon in worthless country where the winds were far too cold for comfort. The Spaniards went back to Mexico.

The Catholic church of Spain, however, was looking for converts, not gold. The explorers went off looking for new lands to conquer, but the church kept sending missionaries to the West and Southwest for the next few hundred years. The missionaries' job was to convert the native peoples to Spain's kind of Christianity. The Spanish didn't seem to care that the people were quite happy with their own way of life and had no desire to change.

In 1776, a second European explorer accidentally saw the Grand Canyon. He was Francisco Tomas Garces, a Spanish missionary. Garces, as you can see, must have been a determined fellow.

Because the native peoples were so difficult to persuade, the missionaries were always in need of help. But it wasn't easy to get more missionaries to come out to the wilds of the Southwest. Some of the more adventurous among those who did come were assigned to find a route connecting the missions in Alta California (southern and central California) with those around Santa Fe (New Mexico). There was already a route from New Spain (Mexico) to Santa Fe, but the only way to reach the Pacific Coast was by a ghastly journey in tiny ships all the way from the southwestern coast of Mexico.

More Accidental Canyon Visitors

And so it was that in 1776 Francisco Thomas Garces, a Spanish missionary, became perhaps the second European to accidentally visit the Grand Canyon. (It had been over two centuries since Cardenas had first seen the Canyon.) Garces must have been a pretty adventurous sort, because he set out alone from the lower Colorado River near what is now Yuma, Arizona to find a route to Santa Fe. With the help of native guides he traveled across hundreds of miles of dry and rugged country until he came to the giant crimson cliffs of the western Grand Canyon near the outlet of Havasu Creek. Here, in the "land of sky blue water," the friendly Havasupai people welcomed him.

After six days with the Havasupai, Garces set off again for Santa Fe on a high and narrow cliff trail which finally led him up to a plateau covered with pinyon and juniper. The next day, from high on the plateau, Garces saw the Grand Canyon. In his diary, he wrote that he was "astonished at the roughness of this country, and at the barrier which nature has fixed therein," through which the "Rio Colorado" (Red River) flowed. He then traveled east into Hopi country, looking for converts. When he arrived, he was told without ceremony to go back where he had come from. Giving up on Santa Fe for the time being, Garces made his way back along the Grand Canyon to the welcoming Havasupai, noting in passing that the area was "a prison of cliffs and canyons." He then returned the way he had come, west along the river.

The next year, another Spanish missionary, Silvestre Velez de Escalante, and two companions tried unsuccessfully to find a more northern route from Santa Fe to Monterey (California). Instead of going directly back to Santa Fe, they decided to go south and enjoy a visit to the Havasupai's "land of sky blue water." However, some Paiutes warned them that they wouldn't be able to cross the Rio Colorado "because it ran through a tremendous gorge and was very deep, and had on both sides extremely high cliffs and rocks." To avoid this obstacle (the Grand Canyon), the little group went east (instead of south) hoping to find the Paiutes' way of crossing the river.

While searching for a crossing point, Escalante and his companions found themselves temporarily stuck in a dead-end side canyon. They named it San Benito Salsipuedes — the last word meaning "get out if you can"! Finally, after several more days on starvation rations of horsemeat and pinyon nuts, they managed to chop some steps in the rock. They led their horses down, lowered their equipment over a cliff, and somehow crossed the river. Then they set off for Santa Fe. They had not discovered a route to the Pacific Coast and they had founded no missions. But they did see part of the Grand Canyon — even if they wished they hadn't.

TRAPPERS AND TRADERS

Garces and Escalante, out looking for new and better ways to increase the membership of the Spanish Catholic church, had accidentally blazed two very important trails to what trappers later called the "Big Canyon." Garces had shown that it wasn't too difficult to cross the lower Rio Colorado's south end and make your way east past the canyon to Hopi country. Escalante found that once you got on the right trail it was possible to cross from the north to the south side of the river further east.

Though most travelers in the Southwest after the time of Garces and Escalante probably knew about these routes, they were more interested in avoiding them than in using them. By the early 1800s, however, trappers and traders began to discover that beavers were doing very well along many rivers in Spanish-governed "New Spain" (which included today's Mexico, New Mexico, Arizona, California, Colorado, and Utah). The trappers also discovered that the Spanish wanted to keep their beaver to themselves. It wasn't until after New Spain became an independent country (Mexico) in 1813 that traders were welcomed into the area.

When word went out that traders could get licenses to trap in the newly-created Mexican republic, fur hunters who called themselves traders began to flood into the Southwest. One of the trappers, James Ohio Pattie, apparently told some hair-raising "Big Canyon" tales of experiences he had while searching for bigger and better beaver.

And "tales" is probably a good word to use, because most trappers either couldn't or wouldn't read or write. Instead, they told their stories to others — who sometimes wrote them up for newspapers. Of course people in the 1800s, just like people today, liked a good, exciting story. So the writers often made the tales as exciting as they could — without thinking too much about what the actual facts were.

When James Ohio Pattie's "Personal Narrative" was published in 1831, this illustration was titled: "Messrs. Pattie and Slover rescued from famish." This "rescue" — like several others Pattie told of — was probably exaggerated quite a bit.

Pattie told his tales to Timothy Flint, who had already published a "biography" of the famous mountain man, Daniel Boone. In 1831, Pattie's *Personal Narrative* was published. In his *Narrative,* Pattie paints a rather colorful picture of himself as evading the jaws of death almost daily, as well as being a killer of grizzlies and rescuer of maidens in distress.

However, he also tells of a trip he made from the Gila River up the "Red River," looking for beaver. The trip wasn't much fun. Pattie said they often had to eat the bark of shrubs. Not only that, they also had to climb a mountain to escape sheer cliffs that came down to the river's edge, then plod through foot-and-a-half deep snow. Pattie went on to tell of many more equally awful experiences of being trapped by or buried in the canyon. Quite a few parts of his tales are suspiciously similar to the reports of previous travelers such as Garces.

But even if Pattie's *Narrative* was put together of bits and pieces from other peoples' stories, it was surprisingly accurate. In those days, when travel in the Southwest was incredibly hard and dangerous, there were lots of good reasons for thinking of the "Big Canyon" as a place to be avoided rather than admired!

Bull-Boats and Beaver Pelts

There were a few other travelers in the Big Canyon area right after Mexico became a republic. One was 19-year-old Kit Carson, who may have seen the canyon in 1829 while on a trapping trip. The other was Jedediah Smith, who managed to make his way from the deserts of the Southwest to California and back several times during his trapping days. Unfortunately, neither of them left any written records of their trips in the area.

Then there was William Henry Ashley, who never saw the Big Canyon, but who was still an important part of its history. Ashley, a well-educated, middle-aged Missouri politician, seems like an unlikely fellow to have been caught up in trapping and river running. In the 1820s, however, trapping was big business — and Ashley had an idea for making a lot of money in the western fur trapping trade.

What he didn't have was experience in the fur business. Ashley got some experience in the trade by going out with people who knew what they were doing. Next, he put an ad in the St. Louis paper. Soon, he was setting out with his own crew (which included guys who looked like the one on this page) to tackle the beaver of the Prairie Chicken River. (This river, now called the Green River, is a major tributary of the Colorado River.) Arriving at the river in the spring of 1825, Ashley split his men into four groups so that they could cover more territory. Because there weren't enough horses to go around, he and several others decided to try their hand at raft-making.

Using buffalo sinews, Ashley and his crew stitched together six buffalo skins and lashed them on a sixteen-foot by seven-foot frame of cottonwood poles. Although they didn't know it, their "bull-boat" would be the first American-built flatboat to make its way down any part of the Colorado River system. Then, down the river they went — with a "captain" who couldn't swim a stroke! They tumbled through a thunderous canyon, today named Flaming Gorge, and then had a chance to catch their breath and put together another "bull-boat." On the river again, they found themselves sucked along between 2000-foot walls toward "a great stone mouth, drinking a river" — now called Lodore Canyon. They capsized several times, but managed to keep their soggy leather boat afloat.

They had an exciting ride down the Green River, but didn't have much luck in trading for beaver pelts. Soon it was time to return to their starting point. After buying some horses from other travelers along the river, they made their way back to see how well the rest of the crew had done. Ashley was happy to find over a hundred men waiting to trade with him. Not only did he collect furs in payment for outfitting the men earlier in the year, but he swapped for more pelts with food and supplies he charged very high prices for. He made a small fortune both that year and the next, then sold out and returned home a rich man. Despite his background and lack of experience, Ashley must have been a tough and daring man. In any case, he definitely gave future explorers a raft of bully river-running ideas!

Some of the "mountain men" who answered Ashley's ad may have looked like this.

Different sized "bull boats" (made of wooden poles with hides stretched over them) were used on many wilderness rivers throughout the West in William Henry Ashley's time. This scene shows bull boats crossing the Missouri River.

GEOLOGISTS AND MAPMAKERS

In 1848 something happened which would soon result in the "Big Canyon" being transformed from a fearsome and ugly gash in the earth to the "Grand Canyon," a celebrated and spectacular wonder of the world. And that something was that in 1848 "New Mexico" (including, remember, today's Arizona, New Mexico, Utah, Colorado, and California) became part of the United States. In looking over its new territories, the U.S. Government noticed right away that all available maps of the vast area had a lot of blank spaces on them.

So the U.S. Government sent some engineers out to survey the boundaries of their new territories and find new wagon roads for the adventurous folks who hoped to settle out West. One lucky young engineer, Lieutenant Joseph Christmas Ives, managed to get himself appointed as official surveyor for both the lower Colorado River and the fabled "Big Canyon." Ives seems to have been a pretty smart fellow. From the time he was appointed, one acquaintance said, "He talked of the Colorado expedition as 'the event of his life,' destined to make fame for his children." And he was right. Ives's expedition to the canyon — which had defeated so many — was to become an historic event. An event which would change people's ideas of the canyon, the river — and the world — forever.

One of the expedition's aims was to find out how far up the river steamboats could go. (By this time, steamboats filled with supplies regularly chugged up and down 440 miles of the lower Colorado between what is now Yuma and the place where the Colorado's huge flow came out of the "Big Canyon.") It was hoped that the river might be used to get supplies or even U.S. Army troops to the new territories. Of course, to check out this idea, the expedition had to have a steamboat.

Ives and the U.S. EXPLORER

It was no easy job to get even a small steamboat from the shipyards of the east coast to the mouth of the Colorado! There were no railroads across the country and no Panama Canal. Ives's EXPLORER, a bright red, 54-foot iron sternwheeler built in Philadelphia, first had to be taken apart and shipped to Panama. There it was taken by rail across the isthmus of Panama. Finally, it was shipped to San Francisco and then taken south by schooner around the tip of Baja California up to the Colorado River delta. Once there, it was carefully put together again and tested. Amazingly, all the parts arrived safely and it still worked.

Ives and his crew probably felt like celebrating when they finally got the U.S. EXPLORER put together on the Colorado River — especially when it still worked!

But finding an inland waterway was only one of the expedition's goals. The U.S. Government also wanted Ives to see that the river and canyon were mapped and drawn, as well as scientifically examined and reported on. To accomplish all this, his large crew included a geologist and an artist/naturalist.

The EXPLORER was finally launched on December 31, 1858. After two months of cutting wood for the boiler and towing the boat off sandbars by hand, the officers, crew, and scientists had traveled 350 miles upriver. As they steamed into spectacular Black Canyon (an area near today's Hoover Dam), they were so busy looking at the scenery that the EXPLORER crashed into an underwater boulder. While the sternwheeler was being repaired, Ives and a couple of his men tried rowing a small boat up the canyon to look for a river (the Virgin) that was supposed to empty into the Colorado nearby. The rapids forced them to tow, rather than row. And the rapids convinced them that the EXPLORER wasn't going to get any farther upstream.

It was now early March. Ives decided to send the EXPLORER back downstream. Then he gathered together several Mojave guides, twenty-two officers and soldiers, three scientists, seventeen packers and trail builders, and 150 mules, and started east up the river's spectacular red gorge. The party made their difficult way upstream through, as Ives described it, "Majestic grandeur, . . . solitude, stillness, subdued light . . . the vastness of every surrounding object produc[ing] an impression of awe . . . ." One of the expedition's "firsts" was their admiring interest in the canyon's awesome scenery. They seem to have been the first travelers to see the "Big Canyon" as something more than an ugly barrier.

A month later, in early April, they found themselves scrambling down a side canyon to a clear, sparkling side stream which they named "Diamond Creek." Here, they first entered what Ives called the "Big Canyon." Dr. John Strong Newberry, the expedition's geologist, was excited about the fact that they were hiking down through fifteen layers of limestone, shale, and sandstone. These formations, Ives wrote, were "perhaps the most splendid exposure of stratified rock that there is in the world." He was right. It was

This determined-looking man is John Wesley Powell. In 1869, Powell and the crew of his first expedition became the first people to run the Colorado River through the Grand Canyon.

also here that the group's artists made the first recorded drawings showing just how rugged the Grand Canyon really was.

But now the going got so rough that Ives and his party were unable to continue up-canyon. Although Havasu Canyon was close by, they couldn't reach it. Instead, they had to make their way up to the high plateau in order to continue east. The expedition tried several times to get back down to the canyon and river, but were forced back by lack of water. They continued across the Little Colorado River and through the Hopi villages east of the canyon. At last, in late June of 1859, they arrived at Fort Defiance, New Mexico loaded with rolls of drawings and maps, plant and animal specimens, rock samples, and notebooks of scientific observations. Although Ives and his group didn't know it yet, they were about to launch the Grand Canyon on its road to worldwide fame as a scenic and geologic wonder.

After returning to the east, Ives organized the expedition's maps, drawings, and observations into a huge, illustrated report. The people who saw the report, especially geologists, were excited about further exploration. But the U.S. Government had no money to spare for more expeditions. It was busy trying to deal with the Civil War. And when the war was over in 1865, there was even less money to spare for mapping and exploring.

John Wesley Powell, Master Mapper

It was not until 1869 that John Wesley Powell, a one-armed Civil War veteran and professor of geology, managed to arrange another major expedition to the Colorado River. Powell, who had read Ives's report and had done extensive field work in the Rocky Mountains, was convinced that "the Grand Canyon of the Colorado [would] give the best geological section on the continent."

In May of 1869 Powell and his crew of nine picked up their four sturdy, specially-designed boats at a point where a new rail line crossed the Green River in Wyoming. After loading thousands of pounds of equipment and supplies into the light sixteen-footer and the three heavy twenty-one-footers, they set out down the Green. A few weeks later one of the heavy boats, which was carrying 2000 pounds of supplies, was smashed beyond repair at "Disaster Falls." On July 17, they passed from the Green into the Colorado River (which they called the "Grand River").

Even with "water, water, all around," there really wasn't "a drop to drink" most of the time because the Colorado was so muddy. The crew spent a fair amount of time looking for creeks flowing down from the plateau. One of the creeks was so filthy and smelly that one man named it the "Dirty Devil." Not too far from that undrinkable stream, though, they came upon a desert paradise. For nearly 150 miles they floated through the smoothly carved red cliffs and lush, green creek deltas of what would later be called Glen Canyon.

Here, a couple of Powell's expedition crew members take time to survey the "Grand River" from a high point above it where they can see the rapids to come.

Just about the time they got used to "paradise" it ended, and they were back to their usual hard life on the river. Cold rain soaked them. The sun scorched their skin. Mosquitoes attacked them. Boats leaked and oars splintered in the roaring rapids. Carrying the heavy boats around rapids and over rocks drained their strength. The cliffs were high. Fish and game were scarce. Meals consisted mostly of flour, coffee, and dried apples. Tempers were short. And there were always measurements to be taken and notes to be written up. Note-taking was Powell's responsibility. It couldn't have been an easy job for a one-armed man who usually had to perch on top of a rock in the wind while writing.

Despite the tough life, they were averaging 30 miles a day down the river. By mid-June they had covered nearly 500 miles. At about this time, Powell wrote: "The walls now are more than a mile in height. . . . The gorge is black and narrow below, red and gray and flaring above . . . the walls, cut in many places by side canyons, seem to be a vast wilderness of rocks. Down in these grand, gloomy depths we glide, ever listening, for the mad waters keep up their roar . . . what there may be ahead we know not; but we listen for falls, and watch for rocks, or stop now and then . . . to admire the gigantic scenery."

In mid-August they camped at the mouth of a beautifully clear stream flowing out of a side canyon on the north side of the river. They named this welcome water source "Bright Angel Creek" (to make up for "Dirty Devil Creek"). While the crew repaired the boats and caught fish, Powell climbed up the granite slope "so high that the men and boats [were] lost in the black depths below, and the dashing river [became] a rippling brook. . . . All about . . . are interesting geological records. The book is open, and I can read as I run."

On August 27 they came to a particularly wild rapid. Three of the tired crew, convinced that running the river through the rapid would be suicide, left the expedition. Powell and his remaining men, leaving a damaged boat behind, shot triumphantly through the "killer" rapids. Unfortunately, the three men who left the expedition expecting to hike out to civilization across the plateau to the north were killed by Paiutes. The Paiutes mistook them for prospectors who had recently murdered one of their women.

After their successful run through the boiling rapids, the crew's excitement faded. Just six miles ahead they faced another gigantic rapid. They tried walking on shore and pulling ("lining") the boats through this new and very dangerous rapid, but one boat broke away with a man still on board. The rest of the men, including Powell, panicked. They jumped into the other boat and tried to follow, but were immediately dumped into the "mad, white waters." The first man, who had gotten through the rapid successfully, managed to haul out the three near-drowned men as they came through.

Three days later, on August 30th, what was left of the expedition pulled out of what Powell was now calling the "Grand Canyon." After fourteen weeks they were at the mouth of the Virgin River (close to what is now Lake Mead). They were the first people — as far as they knew — to have run the river.

Powell was all fired up. He had seen a billion years of earth's geologic history in the canyon's layered walls. He could hardly wait to get together another expedition. His companions decided to continue down the river, but Powell set off for "civilization" with what was left of his notes on the geology and geography of his "Grand Canyon."

Powell's Second Expedition — and Others

After several years of planning, Powell returned in 1871 for his second Colorado River expedition. This time, he brought with him more than just a boat crew. The new expedition included a geographer, an artist/writer, two surveyors, a second geologist (and fossil collector), a photographer, a cook, and a fair number of assistants for each of them.

On this trip Powell added considerably to the U.S. Government's knowledge of both the river and the canyon. While the boats of his second expedition were still on the river, though, another government employee, Lieutenant George M. Wheeler was coming upstream from the Lower Colorado. Wheeler thought

Here's Powell's description of how he managed to get out of the predicament pictured on the previous page (he and one of his expedition members, Bradley, were climbing to a high point to make some mapping observations): "We proceed, stage by stage, until we are nearly to the summit. Here, by making a spring, I . . . grasp an angle of the rock overhead. I find I can get up no farther . . . and cannot reach foothold below. I call to Bradley for help. He finds a way he can get to the rock over my head, but cannot reach me. . . . [Then] it occurs to Bradley to take off his drawers, . . . and swing them down to me. I hug close to the rock, let go with my hand, seize the dangling legs, and . . . am enabled to gain the top." This was quite a feat even for the intrepid Powell who, remember, was one-armed!

the canyon's scenery so outstanding that it would, "as circumstances of transportation permit, attract the denizens of all quarters of the world who in their travels delight to gaze upon the intricacies of nature." Times were a-changing. The natural world and its magnificent scenery were now starting to be appreciated and valued.

In 1880, a geologist from of one of Powell's later survey trips, Clarence Edward Dutton, led his own expedition to the canyon. Dutton later wrote the most important book of the time on the history of the canyon's rock layers. The exotic names of many of the canyon's rock formations are also Dutton's work. He was interested in Asian religions and named many features after eastern gods — for example, Vishnu Temple, Shiva Temple, and Brahma Temple. By the early 1880s, quite a few geologists, geographers, artists, naturalists, photographers, and writers were heading to the canyon to get a piece of the action. The reports of Ives, Powell, Wheeler, and Dutton were luring adventurers and knowledge-seekers to admire and study the canyon. The Grand Canyon itself, now thought to be "without a rival upon the face of the globe," was fast becoming an international "star."

Here, Powell and his crew have taken in their oars so that they won't be smashed as the boats go through a rough and rocky stretch of the river. Powell describes the scene: "There is a descent of perhaps 75 or 80 feet in a third of a mile, and the rushing waters break into great waves on the rocks, and lash themselves into a mad, white foam. . . . Hurled back from a rock, now on this side, now on that . . . our boat is unmanageable, but she cannot sink, and we drift down another hundred yards through breakers — how, we scarcely know."

SETTLERS AND PROSPECTORS

But not everyone who came to the canyon in the late 1800s was looking for adventure or knowledge. Some were looking for homesteads and others were looking for ways to get rich.

A "Wanted" Ferryman

One homesteader who left his name behind in the canyon was John D. Lee. John D., it seems, was not one of the West's more admirable settlers. After participating in a nasty massacre of some emigrants who were not of his religion, even his fellow Mormons would have little to do with him. In 1870 he was ordered to take himself off to the back country of Utah and stay out of the way.

Not too long afterward, though, the church leaders who had exiled him decided he might still be useful in some out-of-the-way place. Utah was short of water, so they were planning to send some groups of settlers out to colonize lands in northern Arizona. The travelers would need a way to get across the Colorado River. So the leaders sent John D. out to the junction of Paria Creek and the Colorado to start a ferry service. Somehow Lee managed to get together a 26-foot ferry boat, the "Colorado," and to scratch a wagon road up the cliff on the south side of the river. It was hard work, but he was probably glad to be out of exile.

As the new settlers made their way to Arizona, Lee ferried them across the river. A little later, he also ferried some of them back again. The church elders' stories of good homesteading land with plenty of water had turned out to be just that — more stories. The fact that Lee himself wasn't one of the West's more trustworthy men didn't keep him from lecturing the disappointed people about their lack of faith. Quite likely he wasn't a very popular fellow. He did, however, have the only ferry on the Colorado, so it was pretty hard to avoid him.

Lee seems to have been a hard worker and to have spent a lot of time trying to convert ferry passengers to his religion. Unfortunately for him, however, he was also a wanted man. Although his fellow Mormons were willing to tolerate him as long as he did what

Mr. John D. Lee may not have been a very law-abiding fellow, but he had the only ferry across the upper Colorado River. Looks like a team of horses (or mules) and a wagon just barely fit!

he was told, the U.S. Government still counted him a murderer because of the massacre years before. In 1875 they caught up with him, tried him, and finally executed him for his crimes. The ferry crossing was used until 1929, when a bridge was built a few miles downstream. Today, most people who run the river through the Grand Canyon put in at Lees Ferry. Which all goes to show that if you want to have something named after you, it helps a lot to be in the right place at the right time!

As the settlers Lee ferried across the Colorado found out, the lands near the Grand Canyon weren't much good for homesteading. The area was vast, but rugged, dry, and far from supply centers. Cattle ranching just didn't succeed near the canyon.

All That Glittered Wasn't Gold

While settlers around the Grand Canyon were giving cattle ranching a try, prospectors and miners were looking for minerals in the canyon. It seemed to them that somewhere in all the canyon's exposed rock there must be enough gold, silver, copper, or whatever to make their fortunes!

For instance, Cass Hite, an optimistic wheeler and dealer, spent two years looking for silver in Glen Canyon. Supposedly the Spanish, and later the Navajos, had worked several places there. But Hite never found any silver. Hite didn't give up completely, though, he just tried his luck elsewhere in the canyon.

Robert Brewster Stanton was an engineer who had surveyed unsuccessfully for a rail line in the canyon. When his railroad plan failed in 1901 Stanton teamed up with Hite, who said there was gold a-plenty in Glen Canyon. Stanton spent a lot of time and money getting a 180-ton dredge to Glen Canyon. But the dredge was a failure. The gold he hoped to pull from the gravel turned out to be in such light flakes it floated out of the dredge. After three weeks of backbreaking work, their monstrous machine produced only $30.15. They tried again. This time they got $36.80. That was the end of that dream.

Gold and silver weren't the only minerals prospectors were looking for around and in the Grand Canyon. Among the hundreds of claims filed were quite a few for copper. Miners tried their luck at the Grand Gulch, Pine Springs, Music Mountain, Last Chance, Lucky Strike, Little Mamie, Highland Mary, and Lost Orphan copper mines. There didn't seem to be much luck hanging around the canyon's claims, though. Instead, there were a lot of prospectors, a few miners, and almost no profits.

Daniel L. Hogan staked his claim to the copper mine he called the "Lost Orphan" in 1893. The mine was located in the Grand Canyon near today's Maricopa Point. Like almost all the copper mines, Hogan's was basically a failure. But the claim did include part of the canyon rim. Hogan later built a small lodge there for tourists. The lodge probably brought in more money than the mine ever had.

All in all, as you can tell, mining in and around the Grand Canyon never really amounted to much. But soon some of the canyon's prospectors were going to be "mining" quite a different kind of "ore." Their starting point would be those rough and rocky trails they had sweated to hack out of the canyon's walls in order to reach their mining claims!

Mining the Canyon wasn't easy for anyone — whether they were looking for gold, silver, copper, or asbestos (which was used for fireproofing theater curtains). Surprisingly, the folks with asbestos mines probably made more money than most other miners! These copper "diggings" probably belonged to Louis Boucher — otherwise known as "the Hermit." William Wallace Bass, a successful asbestos miner and tourist guide, is on the left.

CHAPTER 4

TOURISTS AND RIVER RUNNERS COME TO THE CANYON

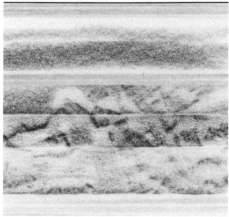

By the 1880s, the Grand Canyon was on the map. Surveyors wanted to keep on mapping it. Prospectors wanted to mine it. A few hardy tourists wanted to visit it. Geologists and naturalists wanted to study it. Artists and photographers wanted to record its beauty. Some people even wanted to run its river. And many of them got their wish!

PROSPECTORS FIND MORE TO MINE THAN MINERALS

Once the Atlantic & Pacific Railroad had made its way across the northern part of the Arizona Territory, people found it a lot easier to get to the Grand Canyon. Not that it was easy, even then. The closest the railroad came to the Canyon was about twenty miles, at Peach Springs. This little settlement had been a camp used by railroad construction crews. It was (and is) about midway between two other rail camps—Kingman and Seligman.

Anyway, in 1883 a few rough-it type sightseers began riding horses down Peach Springs Canyon to Diamond Creek. (The 1858 Ives expedition named both Peach Springs, where they found a single peach tree, and the creek—which was clear and sparkling, like diamonds.) From the creek, visitors could scramble (or bribe their horses to carry them) a rough two miles or so to the rushing Colorado River.

The next year, in 1884, one J.H. Farlee managed to scratch the Grand Canyon's first South Rim wagon trail to Diamond Creek. Mr. Farlee seems to have had tourist dollars in mind right from the start. One of the first things he did after completing the wagon trail to the creek was to build a small "hotel" (some guests called it a shack). Soon, stagecoaches picking up travelers from the A&P rail station in Peach Springs were racketing down the trail three days a week.

It wasn't long, though, before sightseers had other accommodations to choose from. The Peach Springs–Diamond Creek route to the river may have been only a twenty-mile stage ride from the railroad station, but there were much better canyon views to the east. As the trickle of travelers increased, some of the prospectors along the rim began to think that tourists' pockets might be the place to strike it rich.

Several of these would-be miners had already hacked out rough trails to their claims below the Canyon's South Rim. William Wallace Bass, for instance, first came to the Canyon about 1883 to look for the late John D. Lee's "lost gold mine." Instead of gold, he found asbestos and copper. By 1890, he was living on the South Rim close to what is today Havasupai Point and had built a road south to Ashfork.

Mr. Bass Sets Up Camp

About this time, Bass figured that a trail he'd made down to one of his claims might interest some of the Canyon's more hardy visitors. It did — so he put up some tent cabins, got himself a stagecoach, and soon "Bass Camp" was one of the Canyon's most popular "dude ranches."

Guests roughed it at William Wallace Bass's "dude ranch." That's Bass and his dog, Shep, on the right.

At first, the only way to get to Bass Camp was by stage from Williams and Ashfork, a bumpy 75 miles. His guests stayed out of the weather in tent cabins and walked or rode horses and mules along the rim or down the trail into the Canyon. Later, he improved another old Havasupai trail down into the Canyon—all the way to the river. Now his guests had a choice of activities. The most daring could try crossing the river on a cable pulley. The less daring could try the steep climb down into Cataract (Havasu) Canyon to visit the Havasupai people and view the high, blue-green falls. (Some of Bass's mines were across the river. That's why he put in the cable.)

In 1882 one of Bass's more daring visitors was a young music teacher from New York. Two years later she married him. They raised four children at Bass Camp, and Mrs. Bass took three-day walks down to the river to wash clothes! By 1901 Bass had constructed over 50 miles of trail into the Canyon. The "camp" stayed in business until the Basses sold out in 1923. The Canyon's Bass limestone and Bass Trail are named after the enterprising Mr. Bass (though he himself called the route "Mystic Springs Trail").

Another hopeful miner, "Captain" John Hance, also came to the Canyon about 1883. While he was prospecting around the Canyon, Hance homesteaded near today's Grandview Point. Like Bass, he widened what was probably an old Havasupai trail down to the river. He, too, found an asbestos mine on the north side of the river. And, like Bass, he saw that Canyon visitors were going to be his "gold mine." In 1884 he guided his first group down to the river. One person, Mrs. Edward Ayer, was the first female tourist to go down into the Canyon on foot.

In 1885 Hance built the first "hotel" (it had two rooms) on the Canyon's rim, some miles east of Grandview Point. By 1886 he was advertising his guide services and hotel in the Flagstaff newspaper. Later, Hance persuaded the U.S. Postal Service to establish a station at his ranch on the rim, with him as its Postmaster. The station's address was "Tourist, Arizona"!

"Captain" Hance Tells Some Tales

Several years later, the railroad came to the Canyon and the South Rim started building up. Hance, who was a great story-teller and a still-popular tourist guide, was then invited to come and live at Bright Angel Lodge. Until his death in 1919, Hance was one of the Canyon's major attractions. He did his best to keep up his reputation as a "colorful character" by dressing like a prospector and constantly thinking of new tales to tell. He was well known for telling his wild tales in such a way that people often believed him right up to the last unlikely statement.

One story Hance liked to tell was his "fog yarn," which he'd save for times when the Canyon was filled with heavy white clouds. Carrying a pair of snowshoes, he'd stroll over to a group of tourists. "Well, looks like the fog's about right to cross," he'd say. "But I'll get to the North Rim quicker from Yaki Point than from here. Look for my campfire over there tonight." Then he'd wander off again, returning the next day to ask whether anyone had seen his fire. If they said they had, he'd smile and nod. If no one had, he'd say that the fog had been so thick he couldn't see their lights either. Then he'd mention that although the fog was so thick he made good time going over, it had thinned out so much by the time he started back that it was really hard going, like walking on a feather bed. Then he'd excuse himself, saying he was "plumb wore out" and had to go take a nap before supper.

But Bass and Hance weren't the only people who decided to change their lines of work a bit to accommodate the growing number of Canyon visitors. Other miners had also improved some old trails into the Canyon. For example, by 1891 Peter D. Berry and the two Cameron brothers, Ralph and Niles, had widened the Havasupai's old Bright Angel trail as far as Indian Garden. (The springs at Indian Garden were once used by the Havasupai for growing crops.) In 1892, to reach their "Last Chance" copper mine below Grandview Point, the trio built another trail.

Even though it was a 70-mile stage ride from Flagstaff, the partners found that tourists kept dropping in. The trip meant eat-

These photos of "Captain" John Hance telling one of his famous tales give you an idea of what a lively storyteller he must have been.

Louis Boucher was so shy that people called him "the Hermit." Here, he's riding his favorite white mule, Silver Bell.

In the early 1900s, Hermit Camp was certainly no ordinary tourist stop. After staying a while beneath the towering cliffs and above the roaring Colorado River, the Hermit's guests must have had plenty to tell their friends when they returned home!

ing dust, splashing though mud, and having their bones jarred by metal-shod wheels bouncing over the rocky stage trail, but visitors still came. Many were curious to see not only the Canyon but some real "wild west" prospectors. Soon it seemed like a good idea to put up a little hotel to accommodate the travelers and perhaps make a little extra money. So in 1897 the Canyon's first *real* hotel opened — the four-room, two-story log cabin Pete Berry named the "Grandview."

Louis D. Boucher was another miner-turned-tourist-guide. He came to the Canyon from Quebec in 1891 and made camp at Dripping Springs, below today's Hermits Rest. Boucher's trail led from the rim down to Dripping Springs and then down to the river through a canyon now named after him. Louis was a rather quiet fellow and didn't socialize much (probably because he lived so far from other settlements). His nickname was "the Hermit," which is where the name "Hermits Rest" came from. (Hermits Rest is at the end of today's West Rim Drive.)

"The Hermit" built the first tourist cabins near the river where his copper mine was located. He also planted a wonderful garden in the Canyon and an orchard with 75 fruit trees. His guests must have eaten well!

HARD TRAVELIN' TOURISTS DISCOVER THE CANYON

More and more tourists were coming to the Canyon each year. In 1899 there were 900 visitors — quite a difference from 1883's 67 visitors! The guest books from those days give us some idea of what the Canyon's callers thought of their visits. One woman seems to have had a problem with heights, because she wrote: "It scares me to even try to look down into it. My God, I am afraid the whole country will fall into this great hole in the ground." At the other extreme, a rather adventurous couple put their experiences into a few short words: "Went to the river and back; too tired to write more."

But the 900 visitors of 1899 were soon to become many, many more — as soon as the railroad arrived at the Canyon's South Rim in 1901. The railroad made getting to the Canyon a lot easier and a lot cheaper. Instead of paying $20 and riding the jouncing stagecoach all day, people could pay $3.95 and get to the Canyon from Williams in only three hours. Within a few years, the Fred Harvey Company had built a large new hotel, and Grand Canyon Village began to take shape.

These folks gathered on September 17, 1901 to have their photo taken with the first passenger train to arrive in Grand Canyon. The brakeman is the fellow with the billed cap and watch chain in the foreground.

A Funny Thing Happened on the Way to the Rim

Just a year after the railroad came to the South Rim, four men and a "Toledo 8" (a steam-driven automobile) made the first automobile trip to the Canyon from Flagstaff. Like most first trips, this one wasn't easy. According to one of the group, a journalist named Winfield Hogaboom, "the machine worked splendidly — *until* we were out of sight of the assembled populace [of Flagstaff]." There they had their first breakdown. They had planned to arrive at the Canyon at 2 PM that same day they left Flagstaff. The automobile seems to have had other ideas.

After several more problems they discovered that it was getting dark and they were still a long way from the Canyon. Luckily, some cowboys had space for them on the floor of their bunkhouse. After shivering all night without blankets, they found the car's engine had frozen. They built a fire under its boilers and finally got it going again.

Not much later, though, their Toledo 8 refused to go any further. According to a sign on a prospector's cabin nearby, it was only six miles to the Grand Canyon. Oliver Lippincott, the driver,

The first auto to reach the Grand Canyon's South Rim from Flagstaff didn't actually have six wheels! That's a trailer on the back. The driver is Oliver Lippincott; Winfield Hogaboom (who hiked 18 miles to Pete Berry's hotel on the rim after the car broke down) is puffing on his pipe in the trailer.

and the other two passengers elected Mr. Hogaboom to walk the remaining miles to Pete Berry's Grandview Hotel. When he arrived there, eighteen miles later, he told Berry that "the man who put up that sign ought to be killed with a dull hatchet." The rest of the party were soon rescued with Berry's four-horse stagecoach.

A few days later, Hogaboom and two of his companions discovered that, unfortunately, they would be unable to make the return trip with Lippincott. They all, it seemed, had urgent business that required them to leave on the train right away. Lippincott and Berry made the trip back to Flagstaff in a surprising seven hours.

From that time on (1902), the automobile began steadily overtaking the railroad as a means of transportation to the Canyon. By 1926, more people came to the Canyon in cars than by rail. In 1929 over 200,000 people visited the Canyon — and most of them came in cars.

Getting to the Canyon's isolated North Rim was more of a problem. It wasn't until 1907 that people could get from one rim to the other. And then they crossed the Colorado River to Bright Angel Canyon in a cage (big enough for one mule!) strung on a cable. A tourist camp set up at the mouth of Bright Angel Creek later became today's Phantom Ranch.

In the early 1900s — and even today — there was no way to get to the Canyon's North Rim by rail. By 1919 there was a rough dirt road to the North Rim from Kanab, Utah. However, if you wanted to drive from the South Rim to the North, it was a long 600 miles. Today it's still over 200 miles. Yet, if you could string a tight rope from one rim to the other it would be only an average of ten miles long!

Most people who traveled to the Canyon's North Rim in those days were hunters. Visitors could stay in the tent cabins of Wylie's Way Camp where they were provided with mules and guides if they needed them. By 1928, though, Grand Canyon Lodge and more than 100 cabins had been built on the North Rim. During the same year, a rigid suspension bridge across the river was completed, making it a lot easier to get from rim to rim. The Grand Canyon's North Rim was no longer quite so isolated.

It looks like at least one tourist who came to the Canyon in a car wanted to get as close as he could to the view! The car is a Metz; the year is 1914.

RIVER RUNNERS RIDE THE RAPIDS

Although more and more people were going from rim to river and back on the trails prospectors were chopping out, not many people traveled the Colorado River's "trail" through the 277-mile canyon. The few who tried running the river after Powell's trips still weren't doing it for adventure or sightseeing, but rather for specific purposes such as geologic study, trapping, surveying, prospecting, mapping, and so on. It wasn't until the late 1930s that people began going down the Colorado to admire the inner canyon's beauties — and to *willingly* experience the thrills and excitement of river-running. In fact, the number of people known to have run the river didn't reach 100 until 1949!

Powell and his nine companions became the first long-distance Colorado river-runners in 1869. From then on a lot happened in the world of Colorado River running.

For example, Robert Brewster Stanton went down the river in 1889 to survey it for a rail line. Stanton lost several men to death and injury on his expedition. Afterwards, his backers decided a railroad along the river wasn't such a good idea after all. (Later, you remember, Stanton had some more hard luck with an expensive gold dredge that didn't work. Despite all these troubles, his friends said that Stanton still loved the Canyon.)

Then in 1896 George F. Flavell, a trapper, set out from the Green River with a friend to run the Colorado. Flavell's journal tells us what his idea of success was — "There is only one stone we must *not* hit: our Tomb Stone!" According to this definition, their trip must have been a success. They made it all the way to Yuma, and picked up a few beaver pelts along the way.

Galloway Reverses Some Rowers

Another trapper, Nathaniel T. Galloway, not only made it down the river but also figured out a new and safer way to run the rapids. He decided that rowers shouldn't face backward, leading into the rapids with the bow (the front of the boat) — like Powell and all the rest. Instead, Galloway turned the whole technique around by having the rower face forward and put the *stern* (the back of the boat) into the rapids first. This meant the rowers could see where they were going and could guide the boats around rocks and whirlpools. His new technique worked so well that almost all river runners since then have used it.

Between 1900 and 1908 several prospectors safely made the dangerous trip down the roaring Colorado. None of them seemed to find any minerals worth mining. One of them, Arthur R. Sanger, talks in his diary of "terrible rapids" and "mile-high walls," but makes no mention of mining possibilities.

By 1909, however, some adventurous folks were beginning to think about going down the river just to be going down the river. A couple of years later, after several people had done this quite successfully, the Kolb brothers decided to have a go at it.

This 1909 river runner is facing into the rapids, stern first. Compare his method with Powell's, shown in the illustration on pages 36 and 37.

The Kolbs Film a New "Star"

Ellsworth and Emery Kolb were photographers who had been in the Grand Canyon area since 1902. Their river trip was going to be different. They were determined to be the first to record a boat trip down the Colorado on movie film — and they were. The Kolbs' movies and slides of the Canyon helped make them and the Canyon famous. Like Hance, they became "fixtures" at the Canyon. Emery, in fact, lived at the Canyon until his death in 1976 at age 95. The Kolbs' studio, perched on the cliff below Grand Canyon Village, is still a favorite with today's visitors.

Of course, some people started running the Colorado but never finished. And a few were finished by the river. A young couple on their honeymoon, Mr. and Mrs. Glen R. Hyde, were among the latter. In 1928 the Hydes set out — without lifejackets — from Green River, Utah. Three-and-one-half weeks later they stopped at Bright Angel Creek, hiked up to the South Rim, and visited with Emery Kolb. Emery tried to convince them that lifejackets were a must, but they left without the ones he offered them. No one ever saw the Hydes alive again.

From the 1920s on, however, most river-running adventures ended successfully. For instance, Buzz Holstrom became the first man to get his boat through the Canyon alone. The next year, Norman Nevills started the first commercial river-running business. "Nevills Expeditions" were a great success.

After 1938 river running was no longer just for the adventurous few. Today, usually starting at Lees Ferry, river outfitters take people from all over the world through the Colorado's rapids and spectacular scenery in row boats, power boats, and rafts. River running is so popular that the National Park Service has to protect the park by carefully controlling the number of boats and people on the river.

But there's one thing even the National Park Service can't control, and that's a certain characteristic of "river rats." Georgie White, who became the river's first woman outfitter in the 1950s, knew this. The motto painted on her truck said: "Old River Rats never die — they just smell that way."

Here you can see just how determined Ellsworth and Emery Kolb were to photograph the Canyon from every possible angle!

CHAPTER 5

FROM "TERRITORY" TO "NATIONAL PARK"

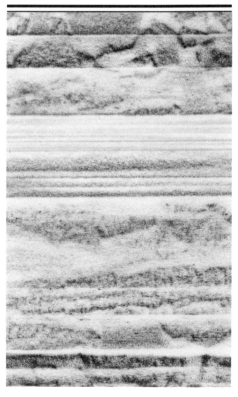

On the preceding pages Polly Patraw, Grand Canyon National Park's first woman naturalist, is shown talking with visitors about the Canyon's unique geological features.

As you can see from all we've talked about up to now, the Grand Canyon area has a long and complicated history. There are different kinds of history, of course. We've already talked a bit about how the Colorado River and the Canyon were formed — that is, about the area's geologic history. (There'll be more about the Canyon's plants, animals, and rocks in the next chapter.) We've also talked about the Canyon's human history. One kind of human history took place before people wrote down things. This is "pre-history." Then there's plain old "history" — which we learn about from what people have written down, told others, made movies of or photographed.

The prehistory of the Grand Canyon area includes what has been discovered about the different groups of native people who lived there over the thousands of years before Europeans came to the area in the 1500s. The history that comes from records people have left behind includes the Canyon experiences of early explorers, settlers, miners, scientists, mappers, photographers, artists, tourists, and even river-runners.

One of the histories of the Grand Canyon we haven't yet talked about, though, is its land-use history. That is, its history as a piece of land "owned" by someone who decides how the land is to be treated. Like all the rest of the Canyon's histories, this history is not a simple one. Today, of course, the area is a national park. But Grand Canyon National Park didn't just appear one day in northern Arizona without any warning. It was a long time in the making. And its story is an important one — as you'll soon see.

WHERE OUR NATIONAL PARKS COME FROM

Today, it's hard to imagine that in the early 1800s the "United States" covered only a little over half the area it does today. In those days, Americans felt that their young country had a long way to go to catch up with the older, more well-established nations. Many Europeans, for example, felt that America was an "uncivilized" and unattractive country. To add insult to injury, some European travelers of the time went home and published statements like this one: "In the four quarters of the globe, who reads an American book? Or goes to an American play? Or looks at an American picture or statue?" So it was no wonder that Americans were interested in making their country look better in the world's eyes.

The U.S. Goes West

Then something happened that began changing people's ideas about themselves as Americans. First, in 1803, the U.S. "bought" a big chunk of land from France. This land — the "Louisiana Purchase" — stretched from the west bank of the Mississippi river to the eastern slopes of the Rocky Mountains. Then, in 1845 the U.S. annexed the lands we now call Texas. The next year the U.S. acquired from Great Britain the lands which are now the states of Washington, Oregon, Idaho, and Montana. And in 1848 Mexico ceded to the U.S. the lands which are now the states of Arizona, New Mexico, Colorado, Utah, and California.

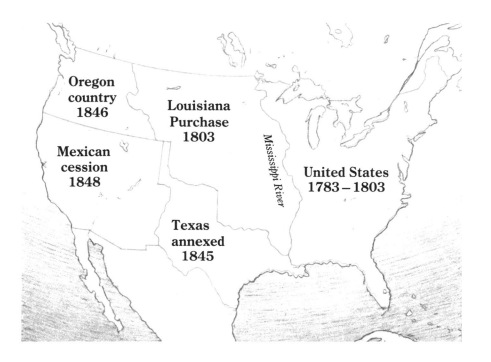

Our country more than tripled its size between 1803 and 1848! The map shows major acquisitions. Between 1783 and 1803, the "United States" was just the land east of the Mississippi River. (Florida was an exception; it wasn't annexed until the early 1800s.)

The new western half of the country was quite different from the eastern half. It was rough, unsettled, wild, and spectacular. People from the eastern half of the U.S. had mixed feelings about these vast new lands. The more adventurous wanted to settle it. Others wanted to mine it or cut down its trees. Some city folk were rather afraid of it. But others admired it — and wanted to travel in it, paint it, draw it, and photograph it.

When admiring travelers to the new western areas of the U.S. returned east with their paintings, photos, drawings, and stories,

Thomas Moran was an artist who first came to the Canyon in 1873 with John Wesley Powell's third expedition. From sketches he made on that trip, Moran produced this fine (and famous) painting, "The Chasm of the Colorado." In his diaries of the journey, Moran called the Canyon ". . . the most awfully grand and impressive scene that I have ever yet seen."

people there began to get the idea that "the West" was really something. (Even if they didn't want to live there themselves!) For instance, the Northwest's Cascade Range had "mountain scenery in quantity and quality sufficient to make half a dozen Switzerlands." Yosemite's Bridal Veil Falls was "vastly finer than any waterfall in Europe." The Sierra redwoods were a wonder greater than any "fragment of human work, broken pillar or sand-worn image half lifted over pathetic desert." And the Grand Canyon was like "a far-off, half-sacred antiquity, some greater Jerusalem, Egypt, Babylon, or India . . . a vision . . . surpassingly beautiful."

The American people of the late 1800s had discovered that their country contained *natural* marvels just as wonderful as Europe's many famous artists, scientists, and historic buildings. Perhaps the U.S. was short on old cities and world-famous writers, but — "In grand natural curiosities and wonders, all other countries combined fall far below it," wrote one well-known journalist in the 1860s.

It was at about this time when a small group of Californians succeeded in persuading the U.S. Congress to set aside Yosemite Valley and a grove of Sierra redwoods *forever* — "for public use, resort and recreation." President Abraham Lincoln signed the Yosemite Act into law in 1864.

In 1872 the national park idea finally got going. In that year, Congress set aside more lands full of natural wonders — Yellowstone National Park. After that, hardly a year went by without a new national park being created. In 1919, the Grand Canyon became the country's fifteenth national park.

In those early days, national park lands were set aside mostly to protect the "natural wonders," "curiosities," "monuments," and "marvels" which were so different from those of Europe. "Public use, resort, and recreation" were also considered, but not quite in the same way we think of public use and recreation today. At that time, many people went to national parks just to look at the scenery — preferably from the porch of a comfortable hotel! It was many years before people began thinking of national parks as being more than spectacular scenery.

Deciding What Needs Protection

But there were some kinds of scenery which the government wasn't yet interested in protecting, even in national parks. Trees, for instance, were seen more as potential houses or fuel than as part of a beautiful landscape. Wild animals were thought of as either "vermin" to be wiped out (wolves, coyotes, foxes, etc.) or "game" to be hunted, killed, and eaten (deer, elk, buffalo, antelope, and so on). It was many years before Congress enacted laws protecting the national parks' plants and animals.

That's the way ideas are, though — they change as people learn more about their subject. The idea of setting aside "national parks" was a good one. And, like all ideas, it has changed as people have learned more about wild and scenic lands. The laws protecting today's national parks protect much more than natural "monuments."

Of course each national park has taken its own road to "parkhood." Sometimes people have fought for many years to get an area declared a national park. Other times it seems to have happened easily and almost overnight. Grand Canyon National Park's story is halfway in between.

In 1905, the Grand Canyon's El Tovar Hotel was one of those comfortable places where tourists could lounge about on the porch and view the scenery. Today's visitors still can!

TEDDY ROOSEVELT — THE CANYON'S CHAMPION

The canyon area's first official designation came in 1893, when it was declared part of a 13,000,000-acre forest reserve. These reserves were to be places where trees were grown like crops. They were not set aside for public recreation or as scenic areas.

Being part of a forest reserve didn't immediately change anything for the Canyon. It went right on becoming more and more famous for its unique and spectacular landscapes. Each year brought more visitors than the last. Then, in 1903, the Canyon had a very important visitor — President Teddy Roosevelt. It was the first time Teddy had visited the Grand Canyon, and he found it to be, as he said, "the most impressive piece of scenery I have ever looked at."

And that's not all he said. In a speech he made at the Canyon during his visit Roosevelt also said, "the Grand Canyon . . . . is a natural wonder which, so far as I know, is in kind absolutely unparalleled throughout the rest of the world. I want to ask you to do one thing in connection with it in your own interest and in the interest of the country . . . Leave it as it is. You cannot improve on it . . . keep it for your children, your children's children, and for all who come after you, as the one great sight which every American . . . should see."

Three years later, Roosevelt created the Grand Canyon Game Reserve. Within the reserve deer, antelope, and other "game" animals were protected. Animals like wolves and coyotes were not. Then, in 1907, the forest reserves became "national forests," thus creating Grand Canyon National Forest. But by that time, Congress had decided that the national forests were not going to be just tree farms — they were also going to be used for mining, hunting, grazing, and recreation.

Meanwhile, many of the people who had visited the Grand Canyon, and some who lived near (and in) it, were thinking serious thoughts about it becoming a national park. Not everyone who lived near the Canyon thought the park was a good idea. Miners and ranchers were worried that they'd be thrown out of the park. Others thought it was a great idea — especially those folks who were getting into the tourist business.

Teddy Roosevelt, of course, was one of those who thought that the Canyon should become a national park. Although he wasn't able to make the Canyon a park immediately, he was able to move it a little further along the road to parkhood in 1908 by declaring the Grand Canyon a national monument.

National monuments, unlike national parks and national forests, were meant to protect areas of "historic or cultural interest" rather than scenery. National monuments could be created by the president, and did not require approval by Congress. What Roosevelt did, in order to include the Grand Canyon as a "historical and cultural" area, was to interpret "historical" as including "geological."

Taken in 1913, this photo shows Teddy Roosevelt on a Grand Canyon camping trip to Cliff Springs, on the North Rim.

A Park at Last!

And so Grand Canyon National Monument jogged along until the Territory of Arizona became a state in 1912. Statehood seemed to get even more people working hard on making the Grand Canyon a national park. Then, in 1916, there were so many national parks that the National Park Service was created to take care of them. By 1917 bills to make the Canyon a park had been introduced in Congress and the new park service director was supporting them. By this time, after years of publicity, many people thought the Canyon was already a park! Finally, in 1919, the year Teddy Roosevelt died, the bills passed Congress and Grand Canyon National Park was created. That year 44,000 people visited the Canyon.

PROTECTING THE CANYON IS A FULL-TIME JOB

By the time the Grand Canyon became a national park, the national park idea had already changed quite a bit. The job of the new National Park Service was not just to protect the scenery, but "to conserve . . . the natural and historic objects and the wildlife . . . and to provide for their enjoyment in such [a way] as to leave them unimpaired for the enjoyment of future generations."

These few words make managing a national park seem simple — but it's not. As the year 2000 approaches, over four million people visit the Grand Canyon each year. All these people want good roads, places to stay, places to eat, trails to walk on, ways of getting around a large park (not everyone can walk long distances), park rangers to help them learn about and enjoy the park, water to drink, and so on. The park has needs, too. It must be protected from too many tramping feet, litter, gasoline fumes, noise, accidental and deliberate damage, and so on.

Ever since the Grand Canyon became a national park in 1919, the National Park Service has had to figure out how to meet all these needs in a way that keeps the Canyon wild and beautiful — and its visitors safe and happy. Of course, it's impossible to please

Native American rock art

everyone. Some visitors want few buildings and roads. Others want more hotels, restaurants, and city-like comforts. A happy medium has yet to be found.

Changes Help Protect the Park

In the middle of all these different ideas of how the park should be run, the park service does its best to do the job Congress has given it. To do its job well, over the years it has occasionally had to make some big changes at the park — changes many people didn't like at first.

One of the changes the National Park Service made was to start a shuttle bus service on the scenic rim roads in order to cut down on automobile traffic and air pollution. In 1974, the shuttles began running and they quickly became very popular. At first, though, some people were angry. They wanted to drive their cars along the rim, even if it meant traffic jams and pollution. But the park service said "No!" They were convinced that people didn't come to the Canyon to sit in traffic jams, they came to enjoy the wide open spaces, clean air, and beautiful scenery. They were right. Once people got used to the shuttles, they liked them a lot better than traffic jams!

Another big change was made in 1987, this time to control the noise pollution caused by sightseeing planes and helicopters flying low over (and even in) the Canyon. For years park visitors had been complaining about the noise, especially in the Grand Canyon Village area. Again, there were some who wanted the noise stopped so they could enjoy the Canyon. And there were some who didn't think the noise was important.

After several years of battling over this problem, it was finally resolved by a federal law which required sightseeing planes and helicopters to fly higher over the Canyon and to avoid some areas. Not everyone was happy. Some Canyon visitors thought the planes should have to fly even higher above the Canyon or should be forbidden to fly over it at all. The owners of the sightseeing-by-air businesses thought they should be able to fly lower. But most Canyon visitors were happy. The noise was much less noticeable.

These are just samples of the kinds of problems the park service has to deal with every year. Some problems, like deciding what methods to use when fighting forest fires in and around the Canyon, are even harder to solve. Should rangers let wildfires (usually caused by lightning) burn or try to put them out? If they let them burn, some wildlife will be killed and some landscapes blackened. But then, afterward, healthier plants will grow. If they put them out, brush and grass pile up year after year until there's danger of a really big fire — one which fire-fighters can't put out and which may spread over a large area. They're still working on this problem.

Rangers Are Natural Resources, Too!

Because Grand Canyon National Park is so large and has so many visitors, there will always be new problems for the park service to solve. But managing a national park certainly isn't all problems. People become park service rangers because they *like* working at national parks. They enjoy talking to park visitors, giving people information about the park, taking visitors on walks and hikes, and giving programs about the park's history, plants and animals, geology, trails, and so on. Next to the Canyon itself, the park's rangers are its greatest natural resource!

Here, an early park interpreter points out some rock art. These figures and designs, called "petroglyphs," were scratched into the rock many hundreds of years ago by Native Americans. Some look like human figures, others look like animals and plants, and still others seem to be abstract designs.

CHAPTER 6

THE CANYON FROM RIM TO RIVER

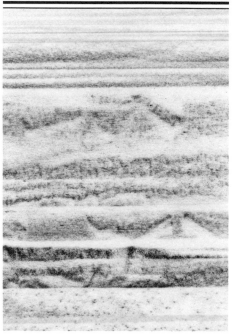

Ringtails prefer to be out and about at night. Notice the large, light-gathering eyes.

On pages 82 and 83, a visitor finds out that once you are tuned in to the Canyon, some of its residents may start tuning in on you!

From rim to river and river to rim, from cottontail to ringtail, from tube-worm to trilobite, from prickly pear to ponderosa pine, and from ancient times to the present day, the Grand Canyon has always been one of nature's most sensationally interesting places. Not only that, exploring the Grand Canyon today can be just as exciting for us as it was for the first naturalists who slogged, scrambled, floated, rode, and marveled their way around and through the Canyon. Just because there are roads, hotels, stores, trails, and rangers in the park doesn't mean that there's nothing left to discover today in the Canyon's natural world.

The Grand Canyon is far more than just incredible scenery. It's the home of thousands of species of plants and animals. And in its many rock layers lie two billion years of the earth's geologic history, not to mention millions of fossils. In fact, everywhere you look in Grand Canyon National Park there are plants and animals, rocks and fossils. They're in the cool, forested highlands of the park's North and South Rims. They're in its colorful desert canyons. They're by the lush banks of creeks and by the Colorado River. Even the steepest and rockiest cliffs have their share.

All of which means that there are plenty of nature-watching finds to go around! Actually, each person who comes to the Canyon sees it a little differently than everyone else. No two people's discoveries are exactly alike — not even if you have an identical twin. Each person's Canyon, and the experiences they have there, are unique.

TUNING IN TO THE CANYON

Because there's so much to see and do in the Canyon's natural world, it's sometimes hard to figure out just how and where to begin. Fortunately for would-be nature-watchers, though, there's an easy way to get started: by "tuning in."

Everyone "tunes in" to what's important to them all the time. You may start the day by "tuning in" to your breakfast — the smell of hot buttered toast, the taste of fresh, cold milk. Next, perhaps, you step outside and tune in to the weather. Is it raining or sunny, cold or warm? Swimming weather or roller-skating weather — t-shirt weather or rainjacket weather? And so on, through the day.

Nature-watching requires some "tuning in," too. And, like many other activities, a little planning ahead is necessary. Just as it's pretty hard to swim at the library, it's pretty hard to enjoy the outdoors from inside a building. At the Canyon, luckily, you're never far from the natural world. Even if you're at Grand Canyon Village (on the South Rim) or Grand Canyon Lodge (on the North Rim), it takes only a few minutes to travel from the Canyon's "indoor world" to its outdoor world of plants, animals, and rocks.

A short walk along the rim can put you in the middle of a forest. A short walk down into the Canyon on the Bright Angel or Kaibab Trail can put you into a desert or next to a rushing stream or in front of some fossils. Once you're away from the various essentials of everyday life — TV and cassette players, lots of people and cars — you can give the Canyon's natural world your full attention.

Everyone is experienced at "tuning in." So, even if the Grand Canyon's natural world is new to you, finding your place in it isn't hard. Lean against a tree, sit on a rock, or just stand quietly for a few minutes and let the sights and sounds and feelings sink in. Tune out the chatter inside your head. Look. Listen. Sniff the air. Feel the sun or the cool breeze. Don't think with words — tune the words out. Blend into the natural scene. Tune in to the Canyon world. Become part of it. Aahh . . .

This is one side of "tuning in" to the Canyon. The other has to do with discovering how the Canyon's plants, animals, and rocks fit together.

But there's no need to wait until you're actually at the Canyon to start making these discoveries. By getting your imagination in gear, you can start checking out the Grand Canyon's plants, animals, and rocks right now. This time, though, you're not going to step into a mechanized time machine. Instead, you're going to put on a backpack and set off on a rim-to-river hike through the natural time machine of the Grand Canyon. Because this is an imaginary adventure, you can go by yourself and move pretty quickly. In real life, you'd be hiking with family or friends and going more slowly.

In spring, many of the Canyon's desert-adapted plants, like this tough, prickly, hedgehog cactus, have bright-colored blossoms.

Anyway, don't be surprised if you meet up with some pretty interesting characters (and creatures) as you tote your pack down the Bright Angel Trail from the South Rim to the Colorado River and back up again!

A TRIP IN A NATURAL TIME MACHINE

The breeze flowing up from the Canyon's depths is pleasantly warm as you settle your backpack comfortably on your hips this bright spring morning. A little nervous about forgetting something, you pull your checklist out of your shirt pocket and run through it again. Water, 1 gallon. Check. Well-broken-in hiking boots. You look down at your old favorites and remember the blisters you got when they were new and you hiked too far in them. High-energy snacks. Check. Yep, you can still reach the pocket where the trail mix and hard candy are. You run quickly down the rest of the list. Check. Check. Check.

On the list this stuff always looks like it's going to weigh a ton and will never all fit into your small backpack. But it does fit, and it still feels pretty light! But, you remind yourself, this is really a luxury trip. There'll be plenty of water along the way and a good trail. On other trips there have sometimes been no trails and no water — and a much heavier pack!

It looks like several other people are just about ready to start down, too. Before you take your first step onto the trail, though, you look again across the Canyon to the rosy-orange, striped cliffs below the North Rim. and down to the Canyon's dark-blue depths where the Colorado River is hidden. It still seems hard to believe that you'll ever actually walk all the way down there — and back up. But you will, you say firmly to yourself as you take a deep breath and step onto the trail.

A Fossil Stop

Almost immediately you leave behind the friendly chatter of the many visitors up on the rim. Looking back for a moment, you notice that many of them look as if they'd like to be starting down the trail, too. Then a raven swoops over, craaaaking loudly, as if to say, "Get on with it, why don't you!" So you do.

The first sharp turn in the trail (called a "switchback") falls behind quickly, and soon you've settled into a comfortable hiking pace. "Hey, this is going to be pretty easy," you think, speeding up. But then you remember that it's nine miles down to the Colorado River, and slow down again to save energy at just about the time you get to the first tunnel. Coming out of the tunnel's coolness into the warm air again, you remember to look for the Havasupai Indian pictographs you heard about at the campfire program yesterday. Yup, there they are. What's left of them after people have tried to destroy them, that is. It makes you mad. "Why do people want to go and ruin things like that?" you wonder. But at about this time, you almost bump into a tall hiker who's stopped to look back up toward the South Rim.

Looking at fossils in the Kaibab limestone.

The wheel-like sea lily fossil is actually a cross-section through the "stalk" part of the organism shown above. Although "sea lilies" look like flowering plants, they're actually related to starfish and sea urchins — so they're animals!

"Oops, sorry," you say.

"It's OK," she says, smiling. "You didn't actually step on me."

"What're you looking at?" you ask.

"Believe it or not, I'm looking at the bottom of a sea," she replies.

"Huh? . . . Oh, yeah, I get it. You mean that gray rock, there. Isn't that Kaibab limestone, the stuff that's the Grand Canyon's top layer? It was once at the bottom of a sea, so it's mostly made of crunched-up and dissolved sea shells, right?"

"How did you know?" she asks, surprised.

"Well, I've been reading a lot about the Grand Canyon. I wanted to know what I'd be seeing on my hike down to the river," you say.

"How would you like to see some fossils that aren't crunched up? They're just around that corner down there."

A few minutes later you're both standing at the end of a short side trail in front of some giant boulders of Kaibab limestone. Then your new friend pulls out a small magnifying glass from her back pocket, hands it to you, and says, "What do you see?"

The first thing you see looks like a tiny wheel about a half-inch across. Your fossil-guide tells you it's part of a 250-million-year-old sea lily. Then you find the remains of a small, fluted shell and some ancient coral. The longer you look, the more fossils you see. "I could look at fossils all day!" you say.

"Uh-oh," your guide says, "that reminds me that I have to get back to work!"

"Work? You work at the Canyon?"

"Yes. I'm a ranger here," she says.

You start to hand the magnifying glass back to her, but she says to keep it because she has several others. You thank her quickly and decide to get going too.

Before you know it, you've walked your way out of the gray limestone layer, down through some reddish limestone, and out the second tunnel. "I don't think I'll ever get tired of this scenery," you say to yourself as you emerge from the tunnel and see still another color of rock.

As you stop for a minute to look around, a couple of hikers behind pass by, and you hear one say, "It's really like walking through time. We've already gone through 270 million years worth in about a half-hour!"

Then the other hiker says something about walking through seas into a desert, but you don't catch most of it because they get too far away.

Right about this time, you notice the rock around you is light brown, sort of sandy-looking, and you're pretty sure it's sandstone. "Oh, yeah, I remember now," you think. "This means that before all those seas, there was a desert of giant dunes here."

A few switchbacks ahead there's a big change from light brown cliffs to bright, orangey-red rocky slopes. And red, you remember from your reading, means that there's iron around somewhere. Sometimes it's right in the red rock and sometimes it's been washed down from the rocks above. Also, cliffs usually mean hard rock and slopes usually mean soft rock.

And that little building ahead means you've reached Mile-and-a-Half Rest House. A trail marker here reads 5714 feet. You've come down over a thousand feet already! The shade feels good,

Hikers can see many of the Canyon's animals and plants along the trail.

Several kinds of jays live at the Canyon. This scrub jay has a whitish throat and gray back — its head, wings, and tail are bright blue. The Steller's jay has a handsome crest and a blue-black head, breast, and shoulders; the rest is bright blue. Pinyon jays look like scrub jays except that they are mostly gray.

and you decide to take a short break for a drink and a snack. While you're resting and looking at the view over several rock layers, you hear some people nearby say they're going to start watching for desert plants pretty soon. "Doesn't look much like a desert here," you say to yourself, looking around at the greenery and the good-sized oaks and firs. You even see a chipmunk and a jay (the kind with a big crest).

Then it's time to get on the trail again. A few minutes later, you turn Two-Mile Corner and start switchbacking steeply down. Time passes quickly, what with watching your feet to keep from stumbling too close to the trail's edge (it's a long way down in lots of places!) and keeping an eye on the scenery down-canyon. Suddenly, Three-Mile Rest House is in front of you. Time for another drink and a few mouthfuls of trail mix. While you're munching and listening to the talk of the other hikers, you learn that this rest stop is famous for its views of something called "The Battleship." That must be it over there. Actually, you think this particular butte looks sort of like a layer cake.

As you're zipping up your pack, you hear people talking about "the Redwall" and "Jacob's Ladder." The Redwall, you know, is another huge layer of limestone. Like the name says, it's red. But you also remember that under the red, it's white. The red is more iron "rust" that rain has washed down onto it from other rocks above. And you can see the brightly-colored Redwall just ahead.

But what's "Jacob's Ladder"? You don't much like the sound of that. Going up and down ladders is not one of your favorite things. When you get to the "ladder" you're happy to see that it's some very steep switchbacks, not a real ladder.

An Oasis

Once this steep part is behind you, it seems only minutes before you get to Indian Garden, with its creek, trees, and even a ranger station. Tents are scattered here and there, and hikers are eating at picnic tables. You find yourself an empty space and get out your lunch. A ranger is talking with a group of people nearby, and you move to the end of your bench to hear them better.

"That's right, it was about 700 years ago that the Havasupai started farming down here," the ranger says. "And not too long ago the water for Grand Canyon Village was piped from here up to the South Rim. Now the water is piped over from Roaring Springs on the Canyon's north side. You've probably seen the pipeline from the trail."

"Yes, we have," one of the hikers says. "But something we haven't seen is bighorn sheep."

The ranger smiles. "Well, you're not the only ones who'd like to see the bighorn. I'm afraid they're pretty shy, though. And this is not where you're likely to see them. You'd have better luck on the way to Plateau Point. That's the kind of rocky, desert area they like. The trail starts right over there."

"Really? Then maybe we'll try it today. We're going to camp here tonight and hike back up to the rim in the morning."

The ranger suggests that Plateau Point is also a good place to look for fossils. Especially tubeworm burrows and trilobite trails.

"Trilobites? What's a trilobite?" one of them asks.

"Sort of horseshoe-crab-like sea creatures which lived hundreds of millions of years ago. They were the ancestors of some of today's insects," the ranger replies. He gives them some directions on where to find the fossils at Plateau Point and wishes them good luck.

Wandering over to the table where you're sitting with some other hikers, the ranger asks, "Seen any wildlife along the trail?"

While you're still trying to decide if you might have time to go after those trilobite trails, a man who looks sort of like your grandfather answers, "As a matter of fact, I did. A mule deer and several rabbits with white tails. And chipmunks."

"So did I," says another. "A coyote, up near the South Rim. A rabbit with extra-long ears and a black tail. And a rather fat, grey, rock squirrel."

Then you add your finds to the list. "Back up near the first rest house I saw a chipmunk and a jay—the kind with a big crest. The ravens weren't exactly on the trail, but they looked like they were keeping an eye on the hikers."

Cliff chipmunks live on both rims and in the canyon. They're small (3 to 4 inches), with boldly striped faces and reddish fur.

tassel-eared
squirrel

Clark's
nutcracker

raven

hairy
woodpecker

mule deer

globe
mallow

Mormon tea

gray fox

porcupine

prairie coneflow

pussytoes

cliffrose

least chipmunk
(North Rim)

great horned owl

pinyon pine

bobcat

Western tiger swallowtail

banana yucca

Colorado 4 o'clock

black-tailed jackrabbit

PLANTS AND ANIMALS YOU MAY SEE ALONG THE RIMS AND IN THE UPPER GRAND CANYON

Illustrated on these pages are just a few of the animals and plants you might see along the rims of the Grand Canyon. Some, such as ravens and mule deer, are common and not as shy of humans as other Canyon animals. They'll be easy to spot. Others are scarce or shy or active only at night. You'll be lucky, for instance, to catch a glimpse of a bobcat, a gray fox, or a tassel-eared squirrel. You're more likely to hear an owl than to see it! But even if you don't find the animals themselves, you'll find traces of their presence — tracks in the dust or snow, torn up pine cones, nests, droppings, and lots more. The closer you look, the more you'll find.

Because plants stay in one place, they're easier to observe, identify, and study at close range. But even plants are full of surprises, have interesting histories, and change with the seasons. Be sure to look at them carefully.

"Probably waiting to see what you were going to have for lunch!" a sunburned woman at the other end of the table says.

"Probably. Like those," you say, pointing to a couple of ravens arguing noisily over some crumbs. "Oh, and just before I got to Indian Garden, I saw a really flashy orange butterfly."

"Like that Monarch over there?" the ranger says quickly, pointing to some bushes nearby.

"That's it. But I thought it would be too hot and dry for butter-flies in the Canyon."

"Butterflies do need moisture, of course. But even though parts of the Canyon are dry, other parts, like here, have water all year. And wherever there's water you'll find lots of plants and animals — including butterflies. Little oases like this are good places to see all kinds of wildlife. Birds, for example, and frogs, and — are you ready for this one? — skunks! Down on the river there are even raccoons. In the hotter, drier parts of the Canyon you'll go through as you head down toward the river, try seeing how many different kinds of lizards you can spot. It's getting pretty warm now, so the best places to look for them will be in the shade of bushes or rocks. If you see one with a couple of snazzy stripes around its neck, you'll know it's a collared lizard.

"And just wait until you get down to the river," the sunburned woman says. "There are some really interesting birds down there. I even saw a great blue heron! And you're right about the skunks. I almost tripped over one by a garbage can last night down at Bright Angel campground. Nothing happened, except that it ran one way and I ran another!"

"Speaking of running, that's what I have to do right now," the ranger says. "Or at least walking. Back to the office, that is. It's somebody else's turn to get away from the telephone and paper-work for a while. So long!"

"And if I don't get a move on, it's going to be too long before I get down to the campground," you say to no one in particular.

"You're about half-way there now," says the man sitting next to you. "You're already down 3000 feet. It's only another 1300 feet and five miles to the river. Quite a nice little stroll."

The bold and striking Western collared lizard, a member of the iguana family, is one of the Canyon's most popular residents. Look for the neat, dark bands of its "collar." Collared lizards with blue throats are male; females may have orange markings on their sides.

"Well, maybe it's a nice little stroll for him," you think, looking at the muscles in his long legs while you hoist your pack onto your back again, "but he's in pretty great shape. So I'm leaving right now so I'll have plenty of time to get there before dark. No trilobite trails for me today, I guess."

Just outside Indian Garden you find yourself in a narrow canyon area near a creek. A close look at the dark brown canyon walls here shows you that they're made of more sandstone. You find your hiking rhythm again. Seas, swamps, beaches, dunes, deserts. Seas, swamps, beaches, dunes, deserts. Layer after layer. Older and older. Walking through time. Walking where water has carved the Canyon. To the river. Before dark, you hope.

You remember hearing earlier that the Anasazi had grown crops and lived in this part of the Canyon hundreds and hundreds of years ago. Because of the water, of course. You watch the creek banks as you walk, hoping to see a dipper bobbing along or maybe even swimming underwater looking for insects to eat.

In summer, the bright yellow and black Western tiger swallowtail is a fairly common sight in many parts of the Canyon, especially near water.

Cactus and a Waterfall

Then, suddenly, there's no more creek. But there are more switchbacks. And cactuses. Round, fat cactuses. Cactuses with arms. And cactuses with flat pads and bright, pink flowers. Lots of stickers. You're in the desert, all right.

And, what's that over there called? Oh, yeah. "Tea." "Mormon tea." A plant made of what looks like real skinny, jointed, green sticks. In the old days the settlers used to boil it up and drink it like tea. Doesn't sound too good right now, but it was probably OK if you didn't have anything else.

Some hikers pass you going uphill. They look sweaty and tired. But they smile and ask you how you like the Devil's Corkscrew.

"As well as I liked Jacob's Ladder," you say, remembering the steep part of the trail below Three-Mile Rest House.

Laughing, they tell you that you'll like them even better when you're going uphill. You're not so sure.

At about this time, the trail picks up the stream again, and then a surprising sight appears — a waterfall! With more butterflies.

Hummingbirds love the color red—probably because red things are often flowers with nectar for them to feed on. This black-chinned "hummer" has a purple throat patch and white breast.

Yellow and black ones. Orange and white ones. And ferns and flowers. Red. Yellow. White. Blue. The red ones have a funny name. But you're too tired to think of it.

"Food. That's what I need. Food. And water," you mumble to yourself while scrabbling in your pack for the trail mix and cookies. Brushing crumbs off your shirt a few minutes later, you notice that you don't really feel tired any more. And you've remembered the name of that red flower. Monkeyflower!

As you look around, you see that you're not surrounded by sandstone any more, but by hard-looking, dark rock. All you can remember about this rock is that it's the oldest rock in the Grand Canyon. You'll ask somebody about it later, at the campground.

ZZZZaaappp! A hummingbird buzzes your red socks, gives you a startled look at nose-height, and then heads for the monkeyflowers. A little startled yourself, you finish zipping up your pack and reluctantly move down the trail away from the cool waterfall area.

Old Rocks and a Big River

In just a few minutes, you find yourself coming up on the Colorado River and the last Rest House before the Bright Angel campground. "Oh, boy! Only a couple more miles to the campground," you say out loud, though only the rocks can hear you. "And the river. Wow! It looks a mile wide. But how wide is it really?"

"I'd say it's about 300 feet wide, here," a voice behind you says.

Startled, you turn around quickly and see your early-morning guide again.

"Oh, hi! What're you doing all the way down here?" you ask, hoping that you hadn't been talking to the rocks too loudly.

"I'm off this afternoon and tomorrow, so I thought I'd come down for a little 'vacation'."

"You call walking all the way down here and back a vacation?"

"Well, I sure wouldn't have thought so when I first started working at Grand Canyon. But now that I've been here a while and done a lot of hiking, it's become one of my favorite things to do. But how are you doing? Enjoying your hike?"

"Yeah, I sure am! For a while I got pretty tired, but that was just because I forgot to eat. But I won't be sorry to get to the campground, that's for sure," you answer.

"Let's head that way now," your new friend says.

"While we're walking, could you tell me something about the Canyon walls down here?"

"Sure. The rock is mostly something called 'schist.' Here's a small piece. Look at it with your magnifying glass."

You pull the magnifier out of your shirt pocket and look closely at the dark grey rock. It sparkles. "The sparkles are bits of mica, aren't they?" you ask.

"Right. Did you know that this particular schist is the oldest rock in the Canyon?"

"Yeah. I read that somewhere. But how old is old?"

Putting the rock down again, she says, "Would you believe almost two billion years old?"

"I'll believe it, I guess. But two billion doesn't mean much to me. It's too big."

"I know what you mean. Let's just say it was a verrrry looooong time ago and let it go at that."

"Sure," you say. "But what I'd really like to know is what it was like here while these rocks were getting to be the way they are today? I mean, was it a desert, an ocean, or what?"

"No one really knows. Because this rock is so old, it's been changed so much that it's hard to tell what it once was. Some geologists think it was lava and shales. One thing we do know, though, is that the rock was once part of a huge mountain range. The mountains were worn down by wind and water, and then all those other layers up there were slowly laid down on top of what was left of the mountains. Eventually the Colorado River sort of ate its way through all the layers down to the mountain range's roots again. So here we are. Standing in the middle of mountains and under seas, and deserts, and swamps, and sand dunes, and beaches, and who knows what else!"

"I'm not really sure how a river can 'eat' its way through all that rock up there," you say.

Grand Canyon rock layers

1 – *Kaibab Limestone*
2 – *Toroweap Formation*
3 – *Coconino Sandstone*
4 – *Hermit Shale*
5 – *Supai Group*
6 – *Redwall Limestone*
7 – *Temple Butte Limestone*
8 – *Muav Limestone*
9 – *Bright Angel Shale*
10 – *Tapeats Sandstone*
11 – *Grand Canyon Supergroup*
12 – *Vishnu*

By this time you've reached the Silver Bridge. The one that hikers use to cross the Colorado. "Look down at the river," your friend says as you start to walk across. "What do you see?"

"A lot of rocks. And some of them are moving."

"That's the story. Whenever water gets moving over land, it takes stuff with it. If there's not much water, it can only move tiny stuff—dirt and sand. The more water there gets to be, the more it pushes along. Even tiny little pieces of dirt and sand can eventually dig out a good-sized stream channel. So you can imagine that when a river gets as big as the Colorado and pushes big rocks and even boulders along, it can dig a really big channel. Like the Grand Canyon!"

"I can believe that, all right. Just look at those hunks of rock move!" you say.

"We'd better get moving, too. It's getting pretty late, and you need to find a campsite. All the best ones will be gone if you get to the campground too late. I'll probably see you there later. I've got to go meet some people right now."

"Sure. So long," you say. "And thanks for all the info."

Walking slowly now—and noticing that the rumbling in your stomach is almost as loud as the river's roar—you make your way along the final stretch to the campground. Luckily, there are still plenty of good spaces left. (You'd reserved a spot in the campground months ago, so you knew that there'd be a space of some sort waiting for you.)

First things first. You slip off your pack and go to fill your water bottles. Then you settle down comfortably and fix yourself a nice big meal. While you're eating, several hikers you saw earlier on the trail pass by with a friendly "Hi!" or stop to talk for a minute or two. Even though it's only twilight by the time you've finished, the thought of stretching out in your sleeping bag starts to sound pretty good. You spread out your groundcloth, toss your mattress and bag on top of it, roll up some extra clothes for a pillow, and crawl in. It's been a long day. You wonder if your legs will be stiff tomorrow. After all, you've just hiked down over 4000 feet! And about two billion years . . . z z z z . . .

Life in the Canyon

Just as you're dropping off, you get the feeling that someone's watching you. Opening your eyes just a little, you sneak a look around. The watcher is lying quietly on a rock. It looks like it's wearing a blue-grey collar, and it has four skinny, muscular legs, and two beady eyes. One eye is staring in your direction. A lizard. You look at each other for a few seconds, but you blink first and the next time you open your eyes it's just before dawn . . . and you're still being watched.

This time the watcher is wearing silky brown fur, four white legs, a long tail and whiskers, and a moustache of bread crumbs. A mouse. A very nervous, twitchy mouse. You lie quietly for several long seconds as it nibbles down the last of the crust. Right then another camper a few feet away sneezes and the last you see of the mouse is a flick of its tail in the brush.

It's time to get up and eat. Your friend of yesterday has promised to answer a few of your questions about the Canyon before you start back up the trail. Your legs are pretty stiff, so you're glad you'll be taking two days to hike back up to the rim.

A short time later, you and your friend are sitting comfortably, listening to the river's roar and watching it rush by. Here and there a sandpiper bobs along at the water's edge, snapping up insects.

"I didn't know there'd be sandpipers here," you say.

"They come every year," your friend says. "Sandpipers like to be near water, where there are usually lots of flying insects and small water creatures. There are plenty of those along the river. And there are lots of other interesting birds you might not expect to see which hang around the river during the warm part of the year — like ducks and herons."

"But sandpipers don't live in the desert parts of the Canyon, right?"

"Right. The birds and other animals living in the desert — or in the forests on the rims — eat different foods. There are even some that don't need to drink water, because they get all they need from their food. Birds can live in more kinds of places than other animals, because they can fly to water. That's why some birds can

If you see a small, lively bird down by the river that bobs as it walks and has light-colored underparts with dark spots, it's probably a spotted sandpiper.

live on the rims, down here by the river, and even in the desert parts of the Canyon."

"Like the ravens."

"Yes. And quite a few others. If you're not a bird, though, it takes you longer to get to water. So you either have to live pretty close to water, like deer and coyotes, or learn to get by mostly on the water in your food, like lizards and snakes."

This starts you to wondering how plants can live in the hot, dry parts of the Canyon—the places where there's no water that you can see. After all, they can't walk or fly to water, can they? So you ask, and your friend answers you with another question.

"Barrel cactuses are pretty juicy, aren't they?"

"Well, yes."

"So they must get some water from somewhere, right?"

Then the word "barrel" gives you an idea, and you say, "Even if they don't get much water very often, they must be able to really suck it up and then store it for a long time!"

"You've got it. They make it last a long time by having thick skin and lots of spines that keep animals from chewing on them."

"And they don't have any leaves. Does that help them save water, too?" you ask.

"Exactly. You usually see trees with good-sized leaves only where there's plenty of water, yes?"

"Yes. Like at Indian Garden, by the river, and along the creeks. But why is that?" you ask.

"It's sort of like the way you lose water by sweating. What I mean is that trees lose water through their leaves. And because they have lots of leaves, they lose lots of water. You drink water and then sweat it off, even if you're just sitting around. Trees take up lots of water through their roots and 'sweat it off' through their leaves. But water's not the only reason there are different plants and animals in different places. How far above sea level it is makes a difference, too. And so does how hot and cold it gets."

"So that's why I saw so many kinds of plants between the rim and here. In some places it's cool and dry, like high up on the rim. Other places are cool and wet, like by the springs and creeks.

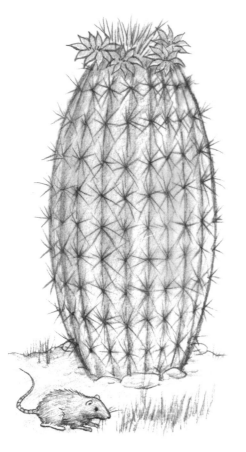

This spiny barrel cactus has "caught" some grass seeds and provided a sheltered place for them to grow. A Western harvest mouse might find this protected, grassy area an ideal place to build a nest.

Then some places are low and sandy and hot. And there are even in-between places where the plants and animals are sort of mixed, right?"

"Uh-huh. Water. Altitude. Temperature. They all affect where and how plants and animals live. This means that when you walk from the rim to the river, you're not just traveling through time from the present to the ancient past. You're also hiking from southern Canada to northern Mexico."

"What? Oh, yeah, I think I get it. The rim's got pine trees and it gets snowy and cold like Canada. And I guess the green places by the creeks and springs are sort of like the northern U.S. The desert parts down low, near here, are hot and dry like parts of Mexico."

"That's the idea. And I'm afraid there's another idea you should be having about now, if you're going to snag a good campsite at Indian Garden," your friend says, standing up and stretching.

"I guess you're right," you say, getting up slowly and carefully. But, hurray, your legs don't seem to be stiff any more! Suddenly, the hike up to Indian Garden starts to look like fun instead of work. And you start wishing there was time to hike up to the North Rim. But there isn't, so you shake hands and say goodbye with a big smile, already thinking about all the places up the trail you want to see more closely.

On the Trail Again

"I wonder," you say to yourself as you head toward the Silver Bridge, "how many kinds of lizards and cactuses I might see." This reminds you to check for your notepad and pen. Yup, in your shirt pocket. "Then there were all those butterflies at the waterfall. Maybe there'll be a swallowtail. I'll try for a sparrow hawk, too — and a golden-mantled ground squirrel. I hope there'll be time tomorrow to look for some fossils at Plateau Point. I'd really like to see a trilobite trail. And maybe this time I'll be able to tell which layers are which and what they once were. Schist. Mountains. Sandstone. Desert dunes. Limestone. Seas. And if I'm really lucky, maybe I'll see . . .

beavertail cactus

canyon wren

Monarch butterfly

Mormon tea

great blue heron

crimson monkeyflower

spotted sandpiper

spotted skunk

red-spotted toad

Western harvest mouse

sacred datura

Utah agave

bighorn sheep

catclaw

Western collared lizard

dipper

ANIMALS AND PLANTS YOU MAY SEE ALONG THE LOWER CANYON AND BY THE COLORADO RIVER

These are only a few of the animals and plants you might see if you venture deep into the Grand Canyon. You'll be very lucky to see a bighorn sheep — and if you do, it'll probably be through the binoculars you're using to scan some high, rocky cliffs! Other critters are much easier to see. Spotted skunks, for example, make regular night-time raids on any garbage that's lying about.

As you hike down into the canyon, you'll notice that the plant communities change. Descending from the rim to the river, you'll go through as many different climates as you would while hiking from Canada to Mexico.

Field guides to the plant and animal life of the Grand Canyon will help you identify the animals you see and give you more information about their habits and behavior.

EXPLORING
THE CANYON ON FOOT

No matter how long or how short, how easy or how hard, Grand Canyon walks and hikes are always adventures. On foot you can get some idea of what early explorers and naturalists saw and experienced. You can even imagine what life may have been like for the Anasazi who called the Canyon home so many hundreds of years ago.

But where to start? Whether you're visiting the North Rim or the South Rim of the Canyon, answering this question can be hard. Not because you have to search hard for a place to start, though. Not at all. The problem is that there are so many places to start from — so many trails to explore!

If you're starting out on a Grand Canyon walk or hike that's going to take you more than a half-hour round trip, here are a few tips from experienced hikers you might want to know. These tips can help you figure out where to walk or hike, how to hike happily and safely, and maybe even get you started thinking about doing the "hike of hikes" sometime — the Grand Canyon rim-to-rim!

Day Hike, Anyone?

Most folks who come to Grand Canyon National Park find themselves taking walks. It's almost impossible not to. All around is some of the world's most magnificent scenery, just begging to be seen up close. Almost everyone enjoys a walk, especially at the Canyon. Sometimes, though, the very same people who enjoy walks so much aren't at all interested in "taking a hike." Why do they feel this way?

Well, for one thing, "hikes" have a reputation of being "difficult" — and most people already have enough difficult things in their lives. When many people think of hikes, they think of muscle-bound men and women, laden like packhorses with enormous, heavy packs, striding with huge boots up and down the steepest mountains with ease. (And probably laughing at the rest of us for being weak little sissies.)

Like most reputations, there is a grain of truth in this image of "hiking." There actually are a few people who fit the description above — but only a very few. For the most part, hikers are just ordinary folks, young and old, from toddlers to senior citizens. Some hike a mile or two now and then, others hike many miles almost every day. But they all agree that hiking is fun!

But what, you may ask, is the difference between a walk and a hike? Well, let's just say that a walk requires no equipment to speak of. You walk to the mailbox. You walk from your campsite to the campfire program. You may walk to school. And so on. When you take a hike, though, you usually take a pack. Now, the pack may be just a fanny pack or small day pack, or it may be a back-pack. The reason for the pack is that you are going to be far enough away from water, food, shelter, clothing, etc., for long enough that you want to have some of these things along with you in case you need them.

Most of the time, these items are very few and don't weigh much. The average day hiker may take along a lunch and snacks, at least two quarts of water, a light jacket, some sunscreen, a flashlight, a hat with a brim, an all-purpose bandanna handkerchief, a bag for litter and garbage, perhaps a pair of binoculars, and, of course, a map. For an overnight backpack, hikers need quite a bit more.

But what we're talking about here is plain old walking and day hiking. For a walk along the rim in Grand Canyon Village, all you may need to plan for is money for a root beer float or a souvenir. For a spectacular hike along the rim out of sight of the village, or down into the Canyon on Bright Angel Trail, however, you'll need to do a bit more planning. So, before getting down to the nitty-gritty of actual trails — that is, where to find them, how long they

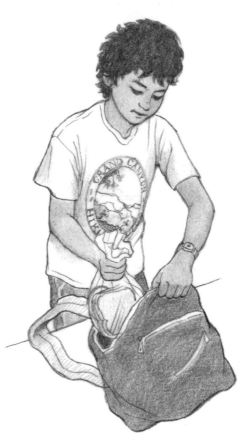

Hikers use a day pack to carry essential items.

DAY PACK
WATER
SNACKS
HAT
JACKET
SUN GLASSES
SUN BLOCK
FLASHLIGHT
BANDANNA
MAP OR
TRAILGUIDE

are, and so on — here are a few hints from experienced hikers on getting day hikes together.

HINT #1.   Plan ahead. Even though the the early explorers often didn't know exactly where they were going, they planned ahead! Their exact destinations may have been something of a mystery to them, but they knew they had to lay their hands on the best information, the best maps, the best food, and the best equipment they could find. They also knew *when* they were going to get back from whatever mysterious destination they set off for — though, unlike most of us today, they were usually thinking in terms of months or even years, rather than hours or days.

Luckily, the best information is easy to find at Grand Canyon. The Visitor Center is full of it — in the form of trail guides, maps, and friendly rangers. But before you head for the trail info, there are a few questions you need to ask yourself. For example, how much time do you have to spend walking or hiking? (When you only have an hour, don't plan a four-mile hike unless you feel like running the whole way.) Will this be the only hike you'll have time for? (If you're staying for a few days, you might want to hike in several different areas.) What kind of shape are you in? (If the longest hike you've taken recently was from the couch to the refrigerator, you'll enjoy yourself more if you plan short, easy walks.) What's the weather like? (When the days are hot even on the rim, a long hike into the hotter canyon might not be the best choice.) If you're planning a hike of more than a mile or two, do you have the right equipment? (Even if you didn't bring a day pack or water bottle, you can get them at the Canyon.)

Once you've figured out the answers to these questions, it's time to look over the best info, maybe talk to a ranger or two, and decide on a trail and a destination. And while you're doing that, don't forget to get yourself a map and/or a trail guide of the area where you'll be hiking!

HINT #2.   Be prepared. For a walk from the car out to a viewpoint, about all you'll usually need (besides whatever you're already wearing) are shoes — and a warm jacket if the weather's cold. For even a short, easy, two-mile hike along the rim or down into the Canyon, though, experienced hikers suggest you take along the following items.

- **A small day pack.**
- **Water.** *In hot weather, take a quart for every two miles you plan to hike. In cold weather, take a pint for each two miles. When you're thirsty in hot weather, drink <u>water</u>. Sweet drinks can make you feel very thirsty, later. Also, start drinking <u>before</u> you feel thirsty. In summer, it's a good idea to drink at least a cup of water every twenty minutes or so.*
- **Comfortable, sturdy, well-broken-in shoes.** *No sandals or thin, "dressy" shoes — even the best trails have plenty of sharp rocks. Tennies are fine. You only need hiking boots if you're going to be hiking hard and long while carrying a load. For longer hikes, take along some moleskin pieces for hot spots. Put the moleskin on <u>before</u> the blisters form!*
- **High-energy snacks.** *Granola bars, fruit, hard, non-meltable candy, sandwiches, cookies, etc., depending on how many hours you're going to be out.*
- **Small plastic bag.** *For litter.*
- **Hat.** *Something with a brim in hot weather. Something that covers your ears in cold weather.*
- **Extra clothes.** *In summer, a light jacket or sweater. In winter, bring several layers — for example, sweater, light or heavy jacket, and windbreaker. Don't forget gloves or mittens if it's cold.*
- **Sunglasses and sunblock.** *These are <u>musts</u>!*
- **Flashlight.** *Especially in winter, when the days are short. And don't forget to put in fresh batteries before you go!*
- **Bandanna.** *A million uses — for example, sweat-mopper, tablecloth (and napkin), muffler (in cold weather), hat (put a knot in each corner), and so on.*
- **Map and/or trail guide.** *You can't tell the players without a program!*

Some items well-prepared day hikers will have in their packs.

This may seem like a lot at first, but after a hike or two you'll toss it all into your day pack automatically. Leave these essentials behind and you'll find out that it's hard to enjoy the Canyon's great views, wildlife, and flowers when you're hungry, thirsty, too cold or hot, and aren't quite sure where you are!

If you like taking photos, by all means take your camera along on hikes. For spotting wildlife, a small pair of 7 × 35 binoculars is handy.

HINT #3. Don't hike alone. Even the most experienced hikers and backpackers seldom hike alone. It's not only more fun to hike with family and friends, it's safer. In case of accident, for instance, someone can go for help. (If possible, someone should always stay with the injured person.)

HINT #4. Always tell someone where you're going and when you're getting back. People seldom get lost or break an ankle at the Canyon, but you never know what might happen. If your family and friends know where you're hiking and you don't show up on time after a hike, it'll be easy to find you if something has happened.

HINT #5. Allow plenty of time for your hike. People who haven't done much hiking (and this includes most folks) need to be especially careful about this. Even if your hike is pretty flat, you're going to go more slowly on the return leg — and of course you'll be taking lots of time out to look at the views, animals, flowers, etc. If you calculate your hiking time using a one-and-one-half-mile-an-hour pace, you should be OK. But if you are hiking down into the Canyon, allow *twice* as much time to hike back out! For example, if you're planning to hike down the Bright Angel trail to the Mile-and-a-Half Rest House (a three-mile round trip), allow yourself one hour for going down and two for coming back up. Another easy way of deciding when to start back is to hike for one-third the time you plan to be out — then turn around. And it probably wouldn't hurt to add in a little more time for enjoying the views. If you get back ahead of schedule, you'll just have all that

Keeping track of the time is absolutely necessary when you're out hiking!

much more time to do something else. It's no fun (and can be dangerous) to find yourself finishing your hike in the dark!

HINT #6. Be adventurous — but not foolish. "Adventure" means different things to different people. If you've never been to the Grand Canyon before, a short walk along a paved rim trail can be a big adventure! So can a two-mile hike down the Bright Angel or North or South Kaibab trails into the Canyon. So can a 25-mile rim-to-rim hike. Trying to find ten different kinds of flowers or birds can be an adventure. Seeing a coyote or a deer can be an adventure. And, at the Canyon, just looking can be an adventure!

There are also a few things that adventure is *not.* Adventure is not, for example, teetering on the edge of the rim — or making your own trail by cutting switchbacks — or throwing rocks off the rim (or anywhere else) — or littering — or trying to hike ten miles when you don't know whether you can hike two miles — or taking cassette players on the trail (except Walkman) — or cutting your initials into trees — or picking flowers — or collecting rocks or fossils (if everybody took a rock, a fossil, or picked a flower, there soon wouldn't be much left for other visitors to enjoy). Anyway, you get the idea.

Many hikers take an extra litter bag so they can do a little cleaning up after visitors who didn't carry out their trash.

Beating the Heat and Keeping Warm

As you can tell from the simple hints above, seeing the Grand Canyon on foot is something just about everyone can enjoy. The trails are many and well-maintained, the views are super, the plants and wildlife are colorful and interesting, and the weather is usually wonderful.

However, the weather can also be a little — er — extreme, shall we say. Summers are very hot down in the Canyon by the river (upwards of 105 degrees F), and often in the high 80s and low 90s on the South Rim. The North Rim is a bit cooler, and is usually in the 70s and 80s during summer. But temperature is only part of the story. In winter, the North Rim is under so much snow that it's closed from November to May. The South Rim stays open all year; however, it gets snow and below-freezing temperatures in winter, too.

There's also the little matter of how far you are above sea level. The South Rim is around 7000 feet above sea level and the North Rim is at about 8000 feet. (The distance you are above sea level is called "altitude.") This means there isn't as much oxygen in the air as there is when you are closer to sea level. As a result, many people find it harder to breathe when they're working hard.

At this higher altitude, people sunburn more easily than they do at sea level. This is because there is less of the earth's atmosphere above you to block the sun's rays.

But these temperature and altitude extremes don't seem to keep people from coming to the Canyon. Millions visit it each year! And most folks spend a lot of time outside during their visit. Smart visitors, though, don't just ignore the heat, cold, and altitude.

If it's hot, they dress in light clothes, use sunblock and wear sunglasses, put on a broad-brimmed hat, drink plenty of water even when they're not hiking, and keep to the shade during the hottest part of the day.

If it's cold, they dress warmly in layers of light-to-medium-weight clothes, put on headgear that covers their ears, take along gloves or mittens, wear sunglasses and sunblock, and drink plenty of water if they're hiking.

If they've just come from a much lower elevation, they give themselves a day or two to get used to the altitude (less oxygen, remember) before taking a long hike. (Too much activity when you're not used to the altitude or heat can make you headachy and sick to your stomach.)

If you do start to feel poorly when it's hot, stop and rest in the shade. Drink plenty of water. And don't start hiking again until you feel better — then start back rather than going on. People who ignore this advice can find themselves with a very unpleasant case

You'll feel energetic for longer on the trail if you snack and drink often. Because your body doesn't start sending "I'm thirsty" messages until it's already lost quite a bit of water, it's a good idea to drink even if you don't feel thirsty.

of heat exhaustion (cold, clammy skin, sick-to-the-stomach feeling) or a very *dangerous* case of heat stroke (hot, dry skin, can't-catch-your-breath-feeling). Heat stroke can kill! A person with heat stroke symptoms needs to lie down and be cooled off without delay. Medical help should be sent for immediately.

In cold weather, if you begin feeling chilly and shivery, or find yourself stumbling or getting careless along the trail, you may be suffering from a lowered body temperature (called "hypothermia"). To fight hypothermia, eat high energy snacks, drink warm liquids, and get warm and dry as soon as possible.

So, don't ignore the weather or the altitude. It's hard to have a really good time while nursing a nasty sunburn or shivering. And even the most spectacular view or the most well-maintained trail won't do much for you if you're thirsty or have a headache. Instead, take it easy, dress for the weather, and have a great time — after all, you're on vacation!

To cool off overheated hikers, have them lie down in the shade of a tree or rock, give them water to drink, and dampen their shirt, face, and hair. As the water evaporates it will cool them. If water is in short supply, give them a drink and at least dampen a bandanna and put it on their head and face. If you're near a shallow stream, you can even have them sit or lie in it!

SOUTH RIM WALKS AND HIKES

So, now you're ready to explore. The trails briefly described here are the Canyon's best trails — that is, the most well-maintained. There are other trails, but they should be used only by strong, experienced hikers. For the most up-to-date information on *all* trails, check with the rangers at the Visitor Center or Back-country Office. On the South Rim, also check the Grand Canyon Natural History Association (NHA) bookstores at the Visitor Center and Yavapai Museum for detailed guides to and maps of the Canyon's trails. On the North Rim, check the NHA bookstore at the Lodge.

Walks and Hikes Near Grand Canyon Village

Walking the rim trail near Grand Canyon Village is probably most people's favorite way to see the Canyon on foot. One reason for this is that there are such incredible views nearly every foot of the

SOUTH RIM TRAIL MAP

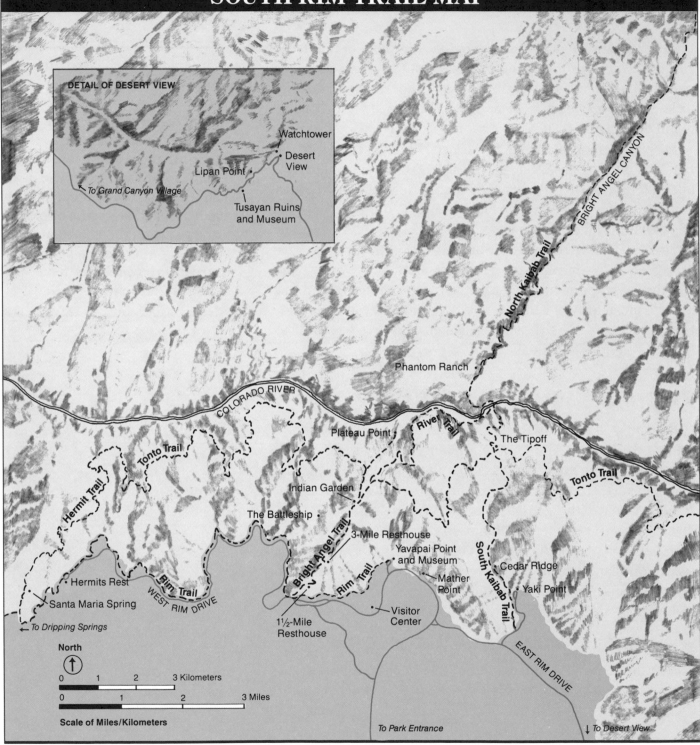

DETAIL OF DESERT VIEW

Watchtower

Desert View

Lipan Point

To Grand Canyon Village

Tusayan Ruins and Museum

BRIGHT ANGEL CANYON

North Kaibab Trail

Phantom Ranch

COLORADO RIVER

Tonto Trail

River Trail

Plateau Point

The Tipoff

Hermit Trail

Indian Garden

Tonto Trail

The Battleship

Bright Angel Trail

3-Mile Resthouse

Yavapai Point and Museum

South Kaibab Trail

Cedar Ridge

Rim Trail

Mather Point

Yaki Point

Hermits Rest

Rim Trail

WEST RIM DRIVE

Santa Maria Spring

Visitor Center

To Dripping Springs

1½-Mile Resthouse

EAST RIM DRIVE

North

0   1   2   3 Kilometers

0   1   2   3 Miles

Scale of Miles/Kilometers

To Park Entrance

↓ To Desert View

way along the rim. Another reason is that the rim trail is nearly flat! And there are nine miles of rim trail to choose your walks from (see map).

THE RIM TRAIL The west end of this nine-mile trail is at Hermits Rest. The east end is at Mather Point. The trail is even *paved* from Yavapai Point, through Grand Canyon Village, to Maricopa Point — a distance of about two miles. The unpaved part of the trail is dirt, but is easy walking. The Visitor Center, by the way, has some illustrated, self-guiding nature trail brochures. (The brochures are also available in boxes along the Rim Trail.) These are good for helping you understand what you're seeing along the way.

During summer, the Canyon Shuttle Bus runs from one end of the trail to the other, stopping at all the major viewpoints. This makes it easy to do any piece of the trail you want. During the rest of the year, people may drive out the rim road and park at any viewpoint. This, too, makes it easy to walk or hike the trail from any point.

You should be sure to include Yavapai Point in one of your first rim walks. At this viewpoint there is a very interesting museum, complete with exhibits, slide shows, movies, books, and canyon rocks you can pick up and look at. There is also a scale model of the Canyon. Also, Yavapai Point is one of the places where rangers meet visitors for walks and talks on canyon geology, fossils, birds, animals, flowers, and history.

BRIGHT ANGEL TRAIL This excellent trail goes all the way to the river and has several shady places to stop and rest along the way. At any time of the year, you'll see quite a few people taking short, medium, or long day hikes down the Bright Angel. (The trail starts just west of Bright Angel Lodge. Follow the pavement past the Kolb Studio, around a corner, and down the hill to the clearly marked trailhead. There are portable restrooms nearby.)

The first good turnaround place on the Bright Angel Trail is Mile-and-a-Half Rest House. A round trip to the rest house is

View of North Rim from Yavapai Point.

Bright Angel Trail.

Trail to Indian Garden.

The Watchtower at Desert View.

three miles, and takes about three hours. (There's usually drinking water at the rest house in summer.) At the trailhead the elevation is about 6800 feet. At the rest house, it's about 5700 feet. Obviously, as you go up 1100 feet on the way back you'll be walking more slowly!

Another good rest and turnaround point is Three-Mile Rest House. As you can tell, the round trip to this rest house and back is six miles. When you arrive at Three-Mile Rest House, you'll have hiked down about 2100 feet! Even if you're in pretty good shape, count on a round trip of about six hours. (There's usually drinking water here in summer, too.)

People who are in really good shape will enjoy the hike to lush Indian Garden, where there are even restrooms. At the Garden you can eat your lunch at a picnic table and talk to a ranger at the ranger station. There's lots of welcome shade. The elevation at Indian Garden is 3764 feet. You've come down about 3100 feet in four-and-one-half miles! Count on a round trip of about nine hours for the nine-mile total.

Most people who go any further down the Bright Angel Trail are either on a mule trip to Plateau Point (about one-and-one-half miles northwest of Indian Garden) or Phantom Ranch — or are backpackers on their way to Phantom Ranch or the North Rim. After you've become an experienced hiker, you may want to do a backpack down to the river — and maybe all the way to the North Rim. (Not all at once, of course!) But backpacks are *serious* trips, requiring much planning and getting in shape. For now, though, what we're talking about is day hiking.

Walks Near Desert View

Desert View is located about 25 miles east of Grand Canyon Village on East Rim Drive. Desert View is a little higher than the village area — about 7400 feet instead of 7000 feet. From the tall Watchtower at Desert View, you can see all the way to the Painted Desert. (See map on p. 112.)

RIM TRAIL There is a short trail along the rim at Desert View. Look for the trail marker at either the tower or the campground. Walking the trail takes fifteen to thirty minutes.

TUSAYAN PUEBLO TRAILS About four miles west of Desert View is an Anasazi pueblo ruin, Tusayan. The trail through Tusayan starts at the museum and winds through the village. Another short trail meanders through the forest where villagers once grew some of their food. Each trail is well-marked with information signs on what you're seeing and takes twenty to thirty minutes to walk.

NORTH RIM WALKS & HIKES

Except for the North Kaibab Trail (which goes doooown to the river and meets the Bright Angel Trail from the South Rim), the North Rim's trails are flat or gently rolling. Some are quite short and take you out to the rim almost before you know it. Others wind through the Kaibab Forest for miles before coming out at some magnificent viewpoint. So, just as on the South Rim, there are trails for everyone — whether stroller or hard hiker.

Walks and Hikes Near Grand Canyon Lodge

Walking the short rim trail near Grand Canyon Lodge is where North Rim visitors usually start getting to know this side of the Canyon. After that, the only problem is deciding which of the several forest and rim trails to try next. Again, the brief descriptions below are for the Canyon's well-maintained trails. And don't let the fact that some of them are rather long discourage you. Just like on the South Rim's Bright Angel Trail, you can go just as far as it suits you and then return the way you came. (See map on page 116.)

BRIGHT ANGEL POINT TRAIL This is usually the first trail North Rim visitors try, and with good reason. It not only introduces you to the Canyon by way of a short, narrow, mostly flat, paved trail — the tired traveler's friend — but it takes you to

View from Bright Angel Point.

NORTH RIM TRAIL MAP

North

0   1   2   3 Kilometers

0   1   2   3 Miles

Scale of Miles/Kilometers

To Park Entrance

Point Imperial

Ken Patrick Trail

Ken Patrick Trail

Uncle Jim Trail

Widforss Trail

Uncle Jim Point

Transept Trail

Grand Canyon
Visitor Center

Grand Canyon Lodge

Roaring Springs

Bright
Angel
Point

TRANSEPT CANYON

Oza Butte

Widforss Point

Cottonwood

HAUNTED CANYON

North Kaibab Trail

BRIGHT ANGEL CANYON

Walhalla Ruins

Angel's Window

Cliff Spring Trail

Cape Royal Trail

To Cape Royal

one of the world's most incredible viewpoints! The whole trail is only a half-mile long and takes about a half-hour. Look for the trail at the log shelter in the Grand Canyon Lodge parking lot (or behind the lodge near the east patio).

TRANSEPT TRAIL The North Rim's next-longest trail in the lodge area takes off from either Grand Canyon Lodge or the campground. It meanders along the rim between lodge and campground for about one-and-one-half miles, giving you a chance to become acquainted with both the forest and the Canyon without having to climb any real hills. A one-way trip takes up to an hour.

UNCLE JIM TRAIL You can get started on this trail at the east end of the North Kaibab Trail parking lot. When you begin this five-mile loop, you'll be on the Ken Patrick Trail for about a mile before you turn south on the loop called the Uncle Jim Trail. The loop is an easy hike, with only a couple of short, steep ups and downs. The shady forest is pleasant in warm weather, and the views of the Canyon from Uncle Jim Point are excellent. From the point, you'll also be able to see the North Kaibab Trail — with its many hikers — switchbacking up through Bright Angel and Roaring Springs Canyons. Hiking time depends on you. If you like lots of time-outs for nature-watching, it could take you about five hours. If you walk steadily, the loop may take only three to three-and-one-half hours.

WIDFORSS TRAIL This is another mostly-flat trail which winds its way through the forest — this time to the rim's Widforss Point. In late spring, summer, and early fall, look for wildflowers as this trail dips gently into little valleys along its way to the rim. A round trip from the Widforss Trail parking lot to the point and back is ten miles. But there's no need to do the whole trail if you prefer short walks. Even a half-mile stroll will put you into a wilderness world that's still much like the one the early explorers found. If you go for the complete round trip, and walk steadily, it'll take about five to six hours. Nature-watchers and photographers will probably need seven to eight hours!

Aspens.

Canyon view from the Widforss Trail.

Mount Hayden from the Ken Patrick Trail.

KEN PATRICK TRAIL This twelve-mile trail stretches from the North Kaibab Trail parking lot to Point Imperial. If you like long walks and have someone to pick you up at one end or the other, this makes a nice day-long (six to eight hours) excursion. The next best thing is to walk a ways west on this trail from Point Imperial — along the rim. This way you get both forest and canyon views.

NORTH KAIBAB TRAIL This is the big one! That is, it goes all the way to the river about 6000 feet below (in about fourteen miles), where people can stay at Phantom Ranch and Bright Angel Campground. From there, hikers can either return the way they came or continue on to the South Rim by way of the Bright Angel Trail, or the South Kaibab Trail.

But you certainly don't have to be going to the river in order to use the North Kaibab Trail. Many, many people day-hike a short — or even long — distance down the trail to get better acquainted with the Canyon. You can go a few feet or a few miles. Whatever you like. If you're in the mood for a few miles, try Roaring Springs.

ROARING SPRINGS All the water for both the North and South Rims comes from Roaring Springs. If you hike down the 3000 feet and five miles to Roaring Springs, you'll see the pumphouse that does most of the work. In the summer, it's often in the 90s at Roaring Springs, so hike up on the rim if you prefer being cool. This is an all-day hike, and takes most people who are in pretty good shape seven to nine hours. It's also a hike that's well worth the effort. Only by going down into the Canyon can you get a really good look at the many colorful layers the Colorado River has exposed.

Trails Near Cape Royal

Twenty-six miles southeast of Grand Canyon Lodge is Cape Royal. Because this viewpoint is at the end of a long "peninsula" (the Walhalla Plateau), the views of the Canyon — especially of some of the "temples" — are even more incredible than most. As a bonus, you can also see the Painted Desert. The road to Cape Royal is excellent, though rather twisty, and there is a paved parking lot there. (See map on page 116.)

CAPE ROYAL TRAIL This short, paved trail takes you first to the famous "Angel's Window," which few photographers visiting the North Rim ever miss. As you continue on to the point after Angel's Window, be sure to look for the natural history information markers along the trail. Although a round trip on this trail is only six-tenths of a mile, it may take you about an hour to complete because there's so much to see. If you try looking while you're walking (which can be dangerous!), instead of stopping to look, the trail takes about 30 minutes.

CLIFF SPRINGS TRAIL This trail takes off across the road to the west from the Angel's Window Overlook (which is on the east side of the road, about three-tenths of a mile before you get to Cape Royal parking lot). Not too far down the trail, you'll pass a small Anasazi ruin. These people, you remember, last lived in and around the Canyon about 950 years ago. There are many Anasazi ruins on the Walhalla Plateau, and even on top of Wotan's Throne — which you can see from Cape Royal. It must have been an interesting climb for those who lived on top of the "throne"! Other settlements have been found on the Colorado River below and just to the east of the plateau. The trail follows a forested ravine to a person-sized boulder under an overhang. Cliff Spring is next to the boulder. A round trip on this trail is just one mile, and takes most folks about one to one-and-one-half hours.

No matter which trail (or trails) you try, you're likely to discover that walks and hikes in Grand Canyon National Park are habit forming! This is probably because you're not only looking at new and spectacular views but at the earth's life story. But that's not all, of course. Along every trail you can't help but meet some of the Canyon's unique plants and animals. So it's no wonder that people come back again and again.

Angel's Window at Cape Royal.

When It Happened

(These dates are approximate and include only those mentioned in this book).

5000 million years ago (5 billion years ago)	No-Earth time.
4600 million years ago	Planet Earth now exists.
70 – 20 million years ago	Colorado Plateau is pushed up.
20 – 10 million years ago	Kaibab Plateau rises out of the Colorado Plateau.
6 – 1.2 million years ago	Colorado River cuts through the Colorado and Kaibab Plateaus and forms the Grand Canyon
60,000 – 12,000 years ago	Ancient hunting and gathering people cross Bering Sea land bridge to North America.
12,000 years ago	Bands of hunting and gathering people come to what is now the southwestern U.S. (Arizona, New Mexico, Colorado, Utah).
4000 years ago	Early hunting and gathering people leave stick figures in Grand Canyon caves as they follow game animals across the southwestern U.S. to better grazing in the eastern U.S.
2500 years ago	Some bands of people begin spending part of their time in and around the Grand Canyon harvesting wild foods and hunting.
2100 – 1300 years ago (100 BC – 700 AD)	The bands of people begin building small villages in and around the Grand Canyon. Today these people are known as the Anasazi or "Ancient Ones." Because the Anasazi of this time made such beautiful baskets they are sometimes also called "Basketmakers."
700 – 1300 AD	The Anasazi build structures of stone, logs, and mud which are several stories high. These large "pueblos" are the reason the Anasazi of the time are sometimes called "Pueblo Indians."
1200	Anasazi build Tusayan village.
1220	Anasazi leave Tusayan village.
1540	While searching for the fabled "golden" cities of Cibola, Garcia Lopez de Cardénas (a Spanish soldier) becomes the first European known to reach what is now called the Grand Canyon.
1560	Bands of people migrate from western Canada to the southwestern U.S. They later become known as Navajos. (See 1860s, below.)
1776	While searching for a route from Yuma (Arizona) to Santa Fe (New Mexico), Francisco Thomas Garcés (a Spanish missionary) becomes the second European known to reach the south side of the Grand Canyon.
1777	While searching for a route from Santa Fe to Monterey (California), Silvestre Veléz de Escalante (another Spanish missionary) gets a view of what is now called Marble Canyon from the north side of the Grand Canyon.

1820s	Trappers and adventurers such as James Ohio Pattie, Kit Carson, William Henry Ashley, and Jedediah Smith try their luck going down the Colorado River by boat through what they call the "Big Canyon."
December 1858	Lt. Joseph Christmas Ives of the U.S. Army Corps of Topographical Engineers launches his steamboat, THE EXPLORER, on the lower Colorado River.
March 1859	Ives manages to get 350 miles up the Colorado, then sends THE EXPLORER back and proceeds on foot with his party to explore the "Big Canyon."
June 1859	Ives and his party arrive at Fort Defiance (New Mexico) with drawings, maps, and notebooks of scientific observations gathered in the "Big Canyon."
1860s	Some bands of the people from western Canada settle near the Grand Canyon among the descendents of the Anasazis (the Hopis). The Hopis called these people "Apaches de Nabahu" ("enemies with cultivated fields"); today, we call them Navajos.
1863	U.S. Territory of Arizona formed.
1865	Civil War ends.
May 1869	John Wesley Powell, a professor of geology, launches an expedition to explore what he calls "the Grand Canyon of the Colorado."
August 1869	Powell's expedition ends at the mouth of the Virgin River (near today's Lake Mead). It is the first to successfully run the Colorado River.
1871	John D. Lee, a Mormon settler, starts the first commercial ferry service across the Colorado River. Today "Lees Ferry" is the place where most river runners start out (the ferry ran until 1929, when a bridge was built across the Colorado River nearby).
	Lt. George M. Wheeler of the U.S. Geological Survey leads an expedition upstream from the lower Colorado River into the "Big Canyon" (which Powell and others were now calling the "Grand Canyon").
1871–72	Powell runs his second expedition down the Colorado River.
1872	Yellowstone becomes the U.S.'s first national park.
1880–81	Clarence Dutton leads an expedition to the "Grand Canyon" and names many of the rock formations after ancient Eastern gods (for example, Shiva Temple, Osiris Temple, and Shinumo Altar).
1882	The Atlantic & Pacific Railroad is completed across the U.S. Territory of Arizona.
1883	A few sightseers come to Peach Springs by rail and ride horses twenty miles down to the Colorado River. A total of 67 people visit the Grand Canyon.
1883–1919	"Captain" John Hance, a prospector, comes to the Canyon. He homesteads near today's Grandview Point, finds an asbestos mine, constructs the Old Hance Trail and New Hance Trail to reach his mine, builds the first "hotel" on the Canyon's rim, and becomes Postmaster for "Tourist," Arizona. In 1906 he moves to Bright Angel Lodge and becomes the Fred Harvey Co.'s "resident old-West character."

EXTRA

1884	J.H. Farlee builds the Canyon's first South Rim wagon trail from Peach Springs down to Diamond Creek, only two miles from the river. He then puts up a very small "hotel" there, the first one in the Canyon.
1889	Robert Brewster Stanton, an engineer, goes down the Colorado River by boat to survey for a rail line. His backers decide the railroad isn't a good idea.
1890–95	Peter D. Berry and Ralph and Niles Cameron widen an old Havasupai trail down Bright Angel Canyon to Indian Garden.
1890–1923	Wm. W. Bass settles near today's Havasupai Point, builds a 75-mile road to Ash Fork, puts up some tent cabins, gets himself a stagecoach, and starts what becomes one of the Canyon's most popular "dude ranches." He also mines copper and asbestos, and builds South and North Bass trails.
1891–1912	Louis D. Boucher, another miner, discovers copper near the river, builds a trail from the rim to his mine, then puts up the first tourist cabins near the river. Because he isn't a very sociable fellow, he's called "the Hermit" ("Hermits Rest" is at the end of today's West Rim Drive.)
1896	George F. Flavell, a trapper, successfully runs the Colorado from the Green River to Yuma, Arizona.
	Nathaniel T. Galloway, another trapper, successfully runs the Colorado River. He also invents a better way to do it — stern first, instead of bow first.
1899	Over 900 people visit the Grand Canyon.
1901	The Santa Fe Railroad begins running from Williams to the South Rim of the Grand Canyon. Grand Canyon Village starts to take shape.
1902	Winfield Hogaboom, a journalist, and some friends make the first automobile trip from Flagstaff to the South Rim of the Grand Canyon.
1902	Photographers Ellsworth and Emery Kolb set up their studio on the Grand Canyon's South Rim.
1903	President Teddy Roosevelt visits the Grand Canyon.
	The North Kaibab Trail is constructed from the Colorado River up Bright Angel Canyon to the North Rim.
1905	Fred Harvey Co. opens El Tovar Hotel in Grand Canyon Village.
1906	President Teddy Roosevelt creates the Grand Canyon Game Reserve.
1907	The first tourists cross the river to the north side in a cage strung on a cable. A tourist camp which later becomes Phantom Ranch is set up at the mouth of Bright Angel Canyon.
	All Forest Reserves, including Grand Canyon, become National Forests.
1908	President Teddy Roosevelt creates Grand Canyon National Monument.
1912	The Territory of Arizona becomes a state.

EXTRA

1917	Tourists begin staying at Wylie's Way Camp on the North Rim.
1919	A rough dirt road is completed from Kanab, Utah to the Grand Canyon's North Rim.
All 1919	The Grand Canyon becomes the U.S.'s fifteenth national park.
	Over 44,000 people visit Grand Canyon National Park.
1922	Fred Harvey Co. builds Phantom Ranch as overnight stop for riders on mule trips from the South Rim to the river and the North Rim.
1928	Grand Canyon Lodge is built on the North Rim and the North and South Kaibab Trails are completed.
	A rigid suspension bridge is built across the river near Bright Angel Canyon to connect the North and South Kaibab Trails.
1929	Over 200,000 people visit the Grand Canyon.
1936	Hoover Dam is built on the Colorado River outside the park's western border, creating Lake Mead. Water from the Lake backs up into the Grand Canyon.
	Over 300,000 people visit the Grand Canyon.
1938	Norman Nevills starts the first commercial river-running business.
1949	The number of people who have run the Colorado River through the Grand Canyon reaches 100.
1955	Georgie White becomes the first woman to start a commercial river-running business.
1956	Over one million people visit Grand Canyon.
1963	Glen Canyon Dam is built on the Colorado River, creating Lake Powell east of Lees Ferry and drowning beautiful Glen Canyon.
1974	To get rid of traffic jams, summer shuttle bus service begins on the Grand Canyon's South Rim.
1976	More than three million people visit Grand Canyon.
1987	To control noise, a new federal regulation requires sightseeing planes and helicopters to fly higher over the Canyon and to avoid some areas.
1989	More than four million people visit Grand Canyon.

Books About the Grand Canyon

Babbitt, Bruce (editor). *GRAND CANYON: An Anthology*. Flagstaff, AZ: Northland Press, 1978. (All ages.)
Explorers, artists, tourists, scientists, and adventurers tell their stories about the Grand Canyon.

Brown, Bryan T., Steven W. Carothers, & R. Roy Johnson. *GRAND CANYON BIRDS: Historical Notes, Natural History, & Ecology*. Tucson, AZ: University of Arizona Press, 1987. (All ages.)
A field guide as well as an interesting history of birds and bird-watchers at the Grand Canyon.

Collier, Michael. *AN INTRODUCTION TO GRAND CANYON GEOLOGY*. Grand Canyon, AZ: Grand Canyon Natural History Association, 1980. (All ages.)
Learn about the Canyon's rocks and layers from this small book and its colorful photos and illustrations.

Darton, N.H. *STORY OF THE GRAND CANYON: How It Was Made*. Revised & enlarged from 1917 edition. Grand Canyon, AZ: Fred Harvey, 1984. (All ages.)
This booklet helps you understand what you're seeing from the South Rim's viewpoints.

Evans, Edna. *TALES FROM THE GRAND CANYON: Some True, Some Tall*. Flagstaff, AZ: Northland Press, 1985. (All ages.)
The title of this book tells you what it's about — and some of the tales are pretty funny.

Goff, John S. *ARIZONA: An Illustrated History of the Grand Canyon State*. Northridge, CA: Windsor Publications, Inc., 1988. (Young people.)
This book will fill you in on the history of the lands around the Grand Canyon.

Granger, Byrd H. *GRAND CANYON PLACE NAMES*. Tucson, AZ: University of Arizona Press, 1960. (All ages.)
If you'd like to know how Phantom Ranch and Sockdolager Rapids got their names, try this booklet.

Hoffmeister, Donald F. *MAMMALS OF GRAND CANYON*. Urbana, IL: University of Illinois Press, 1971. (All ages.)
A field book with lots of interesting drawings and maps of where the Canyon's mammals are found.

Hughes, J. Donald. *IN THE HOUSE OF STONE & LIGHT:A Human History of the Grand Canyon*. Grand Canyon, AZ: Grand Canyon Natural History Association, 1978. (All ages.)
Using lots of great photos, this detailed book tells you about people at the Grand Canyon — the early hunters, the explorers and settlers, the scientists and artists, the tourists and river runners, and even the park rangers.

Lavender, David. *COLORADO RIVER COUNTRY*. New York, NY: E.P. Dutton, Inc., 1982. (All ages.)
A lively history of people and places around the Colorado River.

————. *RIVER RUNNERS OF THE GRAND CANYON*. Grand Canyon, AZ: Grand Canyon Natural History Association & University of Arizona Press, 1985. (All ages.)
Exciting, true stories of Colorado river-running through the Grand Canyon.

Lister, Florence C. & Robert H. *THOSE WHO CAME BEFORE*. Tucson, AZ: Southwest Parks & Monuments Association & University of Arizona Press, 1983. (All ages.)
A book about how and where the native people of the southwest lived, and what they left behind in the areas which are now national parks and monuments — including the Grand Canyon.

McAdams, Cliff. *GRAND CANYON NATIONAL PARK: Guide & Reference Book*. Boulder, CO: Pruett Publishing Co., 1981. (All ages.)

This small guidebook gives you a quick once-over of canyon history, plants and animals, hiking, river running, and places you can explore easily.

Miller, Donald M., Robert A. Young, Thomas W. Gatlin, & John A. Richardson. *AMPHIBIANS & REPTILES OF THE GRAND CANYON*. Grand Canyon, AZ: Grand Canyon Natural History Association, 1982. (All ages.)

Learn about the Grand Canyon's lizards and snakes from the photos, drawings, and range maps in this scientific monograph.

Stokes, William Lee. *SCENES OF THE PLATEAU LANDS & HOW THEY CAME TO BE*. Salt Lake City, UT: Publishers Press, 1969. (All ages.)

If you've ever wondered what made the mesas and buttes, canyons and spires, sand dunes and petrified forests in and around the Grand Canyon area, this book (with its clear and simple drawings) is for you.

Thayer, Dave. *A GUIDE TO GRAND CANYON GEOLOGY ALONG BRIGHT ANGEL TRAIL*. Grand Canyon, AZ: Grand Canyon Natural History Association, 1986. (All ages.)

Lots of photos and drawings, along with easy-to-read text, make this trail guide a must for anyone interested in hiking the Bright Angel Trail.

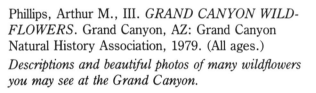

Phillips, Arthur M., III. *GRAND CANYON WILDFLOWERS*. Grand Canyon, AZ: Grand Canyon Natural History Association, 1979. (All ages.)

Descriptions and beautiful photos of many wildflowers you may see at the Grand Canyon.

Redfern, Ron. *CORRIDORS OF TIME: 1,700,000,000 Years of Earth at Grand Canyon*. New York, NY: Times Books, 1980. (All ages.)

This spectacular book is full of wonderful color photos and illustrations of the Grand Canyon's natural and geologic history.

Schullery, Paul (editor). *THE GRAND CANYON: Early Impressions*. Boulder, CO: Colorado Associated University Press, 1981. (All ages.)

Some of the Grand Canyon's early visitors tell about their interesting (and often humorous) trips.

Smith, Don. *THE GRAND CANYON: Journey Through Time*. Mahway, NJ: Troll Associates, 1976. (Young people.)

A quick look at the Canyon's geologic history.

Underhill, Ruth. *WORKADAY LIFE OF THE PUEBLOS*. Phoenix, AZ: Dept. of the Interior, Bureau of Indian Affairs, 1954. (All ages.)

A fascinating description of pueblo life — how people worked, what they ate, what they wore, and the games they played.

Whitney, Stephen. *A FIELD GUIDE TO THE GRAND CANYON*. New York, NY: Quill, 1982. (All ages.)

This excellent field guide, with its beautiful, full-color illustrations, covers the Canyon's plants, animals, geology, and human history — and it also gets you started hiking and exploring.

Winks, Honor L. *THE COLORADO*. Lexington, MA: Silver Press, 1980. (Young people.)

A short history of the Colorado River.

Canyon Sketchpad

Find and sketch at least one item in each group listed below. Whenever possible identify and label what you have drawn to create a permanent record of your discoveries at Grand Canyon. Any park ranger will be glad to help you with identifications.

Animal track:

(A good time to look for these is after a rain. Look closely at the track to see if you can learn more about the animal. What direction was it going? Was it walking or running? Was it alone? Can you find any other signs of its presence?)

Your Name _____   Date _____

Flowering plant:
(You'll find the greatest variety in early autumn, but you should
be able to find *something* in bloom at any time of year.)

Your Name _____ Date _____

Plateau or "temple" within the Canyon:
(Many of these "islands" have exotic names like Vishnu Temple and Zoroaster Temple.)

Your Name ＿＿＿＿＿＿＿＿＿＿＿＿＿＿   Date ＿＿＿＿＿＿＿＿＿

Pine tree on or near the rim:
(The tree's cones and needle bundles will help you identify it.)

Your Name _____ Date _____

Cactus:

(Cactus spines are actually leaves, modified to reduce water loss. What other function might they serve? Look closely at how the spines are arranged. But take care not to bump into your subject!)

Your Name _____ Date _____

Fossil:

(Look for fossils in the rocks along the West Rim Trail near the 'Worship Site' or visit Yavapai Museum and the Rim Trail near it.)

Your Name _____ Date _____

Bird:

(You'll have plenty of "models" if you sit quietly for a few minutes among some rocks or trees. Can you tell what the bird eats by watching its behavior?)

Your Name _____ Date _____

Mammal:

(These critters are shy, but patience — and quiet — will get you an interesting subject. You'll see the greatest variety of mammals and the most activity around dawn and dusk.)

Your Name _____ Date _____

Reptile:
(Because they cannot control their body temperature, reptiles move from sun to shade to stay comfortable. Look for them in shady spots on hot days; in sunny spots on cold days. Lizards seem to be forever on the move and snakes are good at camouflage. So, look sharp!)

Your Name _____ Date _____

Insect:
> (These are the most numerous animals you'll find. In fact, if you just sit still, *they'll* find *you.*)

Your Name _____ Date _____

Canyon Crossword

Use the information you've learned by reading this book to complete
the crossword puzzle below.

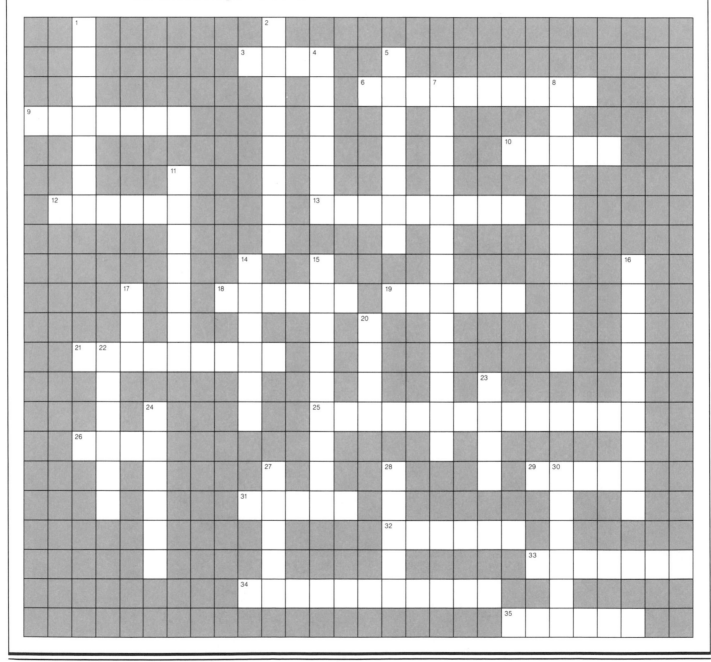

ACTIVITY

ACROSS

3—Early Canyon photographer
6—Ancient picture painted on rock
9—Remains in rock of ancient animals
10—Primary carver of the canyon
12—The hole through which the Anasazi first entered this world
13—Arizona before it became a state
18—Tassel-eared squirrel found on North Rim
19—Indians who came to Canyon after Anasazi
21—Used to date ancient ruins (two words)
25—President who made Grand Canyon a national park (two words)
26—Ancient ceremonial room
29—Country that sent first European explorers
31—Large black bird common at Canyon
32—Thorny plant found in canyon
33—Study of how the earth was formed
34—Popular trail from Rim to River (two words)
35—Ancient spear-throwing stick

DOWN

1—First people to live in Grand Canyon
2—Name of river in Grand Canyon
4—Container woven by Indians
5—Large sheep living in canyon
7—Company offering trips back in time (two words)
8—Ancient picture carved in rock
11—Tree common on canyon rim
14—Offers help to park visitors
15—Rock made of compressed sand dunes
16—Rock made of remains of sea creatures
17—Began ferry service across Colorado River
20—Mineral that prospectors hoped to find
22—Where river flows over boulders
23—Present-day descendants of Anasazi
24—Deep gully carved by river
27—Primary carver of the canyon
28—Plant used by Indians as food and for its fibers
30—Explored Colorado River in 1869

ANSWERS

DOWN
1—ANASAZI
2—COLORADO
4—BASKET
5—BIGHORN
7—TIMETRAVELERS
8—PETROGLYPH
11—JUNIPER
14—RANGER
15—SANDSTONE
16—LIMESTONE
17—LEE
20—GOLD
22—RAPIDS
23—HOPI
24—CANYON
27—WATER
28—YUCCA
30—POWELL

ACROSS
3—KOLB
6—PICTOGRAPH
9—FOSSILS
10—WATER
12—SIPAPU
13—TERRITORY
18—KAIBAB
19—NAVAJO
21—TREERINGS
25—TEDDYROOSEVELT
26—KIVA
29—SPAIN
31—RAVEN
32—CACTUS
33—GEOLOGY
34—BRIGHTANGEL
35—ATLATL

Mail from the Past

Imagine that you are
A) visiting an Anasazi family living at the Grand Canyon 900 years ago.
OR

B) a member of John Wesley Powell's expedition down the Colorado River in 1869.

Write a letter to a friend or family member back home, describing your daily life.
Here are a few questions to help you get started:

■ Where were you when you woke up this morning? Describe the setting.

_____

■ What did you eat for breakfast? lunch? dinner? Where did this food come from?

_____

■ What are you wearing?

_____

■ What did you do today?

_____

■ How did you get from one place to another?

_____

■ Describe the most memorable thing you saw today.

_____

■ Describe the tools in your tool kit or the supplies you have with you.

_____

■ Is life more fun or more work than "back home"?

_____

Date _____

Dear _____,

_____

_____

_____

_____

_____

_____

_____

_____

_____

_____

_____

_____

Signature _____

Fold a Raven

Follow the diagrams below to create a raven from a square piece of paper. Your paper should be at least 8 inches square, but a piece 18 inches square will make a raven about life size. If you like, you can carefully cut out the printed square on the next page and fold it according to the instructions given below.

Begin with a square piece of paper.

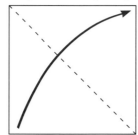

Fold diagonally.

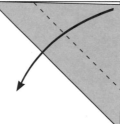

Fold upper half back.

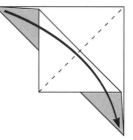

Fold in half.

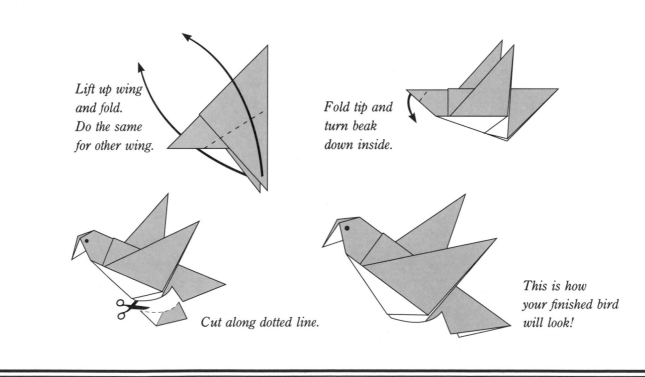

Lift up wing and fold. Do the same for other wing.

Fold tip and turn beak down inside.

Cut along dotted line.

This is how your finished bird will look!

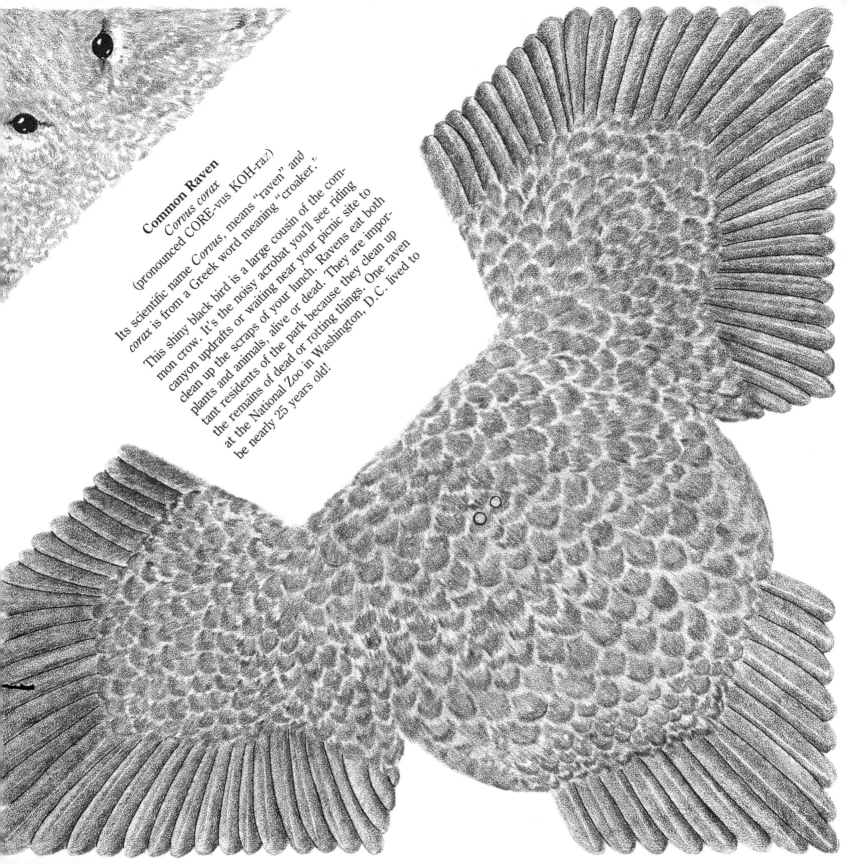

Common Raven
Corvus corax
(pronounced CORE-vus KOH-raz)

Its scientific name *Corvus*, means "raven" and *corax* is from a Greek word meaning "croaker."

This shiny black bird is a large cousin of the common crow. It's the noisy acrobat you'll see riding canyon updrafts or waiting near your picnic site to clean up the scraps of your lunch. Ravens eat both plants and animals, alive or dead. They are important residents of the park because they clean up the remains of dead or rotting things. One raven at the National Zoo in Washington, D.C. lived to be nearly 25 years old!

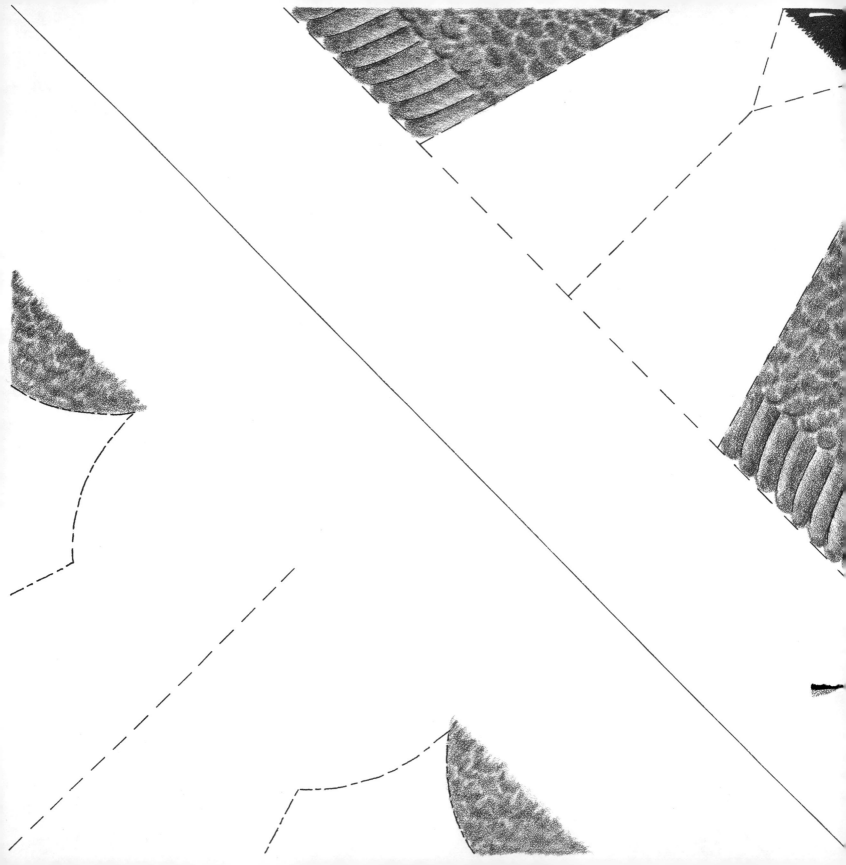

ABOUT THE AUTHOR AND ARTIST

About the Author

Lynne Foster is the author of *Mountaineering Basics* and *Adventuring in the California Desert.* For young readers, Lynne has written *Take a Hike,* a beginner's guide to hiking and backpacking. A former microbiologist and English teacher, she lives in Riverside, California.

About the Artist

Margaret Sanfilippo was born and educated in California. She graduated from San Jose State University, and has studied at San Francisco's Academy of Art. Margaret has been illustrating children's books for 12 years, with a special emphasis on historical themes. She now resides in Palo Alto, California.

PUBLICATIONS

Other Publications available from
GRAND CANYON NATURAL HISTORY ASSOCIATION:

BOOKS

ALONG THE RIM by Nancy Loving. A brief discussion of plant and animal life on the South Rim, and guide to points along East and West rim drives from Desert View to Hermits Rest. 56 full-color and black-and-white photographs, four maps, landmark keys. 52 pp. $2.95

GUIDE TO GRAND CANYON GEOLOGY ALONG BRIGHT ANGEL TRAIL by David Thayer. This lucid explanation of Grand Canyon geology contains 30 photos, 30 line drawings, and 5 section maps of Bright Angel Trail. 6″ × 8½″ wirebound. 100 pp. $8.95

GUIDE TO GRAND CANYON VILLAGE HISTORIC DISTRICT by Timothy Manns. Illustrated booklet describing historic buildings in Grand Canyon Village on the South Rim. 24 pp. $2.50

IN THE HOUSE OF STONE AND LIGHT by J. Donald Hughes. Detailed look at the human history of Grand Canyon before and after it became a national park. Historic photographs. 137 pp. $9.50

INTRODUCTION TO GRAND CANYON GEOLOGY by Michael Collier. The story of Grand Canyon geology in lay terms. 40 color plates. 42 pp. $4.00 pb, $7.50 hc

JAPANESE GUIDE TO THE GRAND CANYON by Masahiro Ohta. Introductory guide to Grand Canyon includes a map of the area. Written in Japanese specifically for Japanese visitors. 13 color plates. 26 pp. $5.00

JOHN WESLEY POWELL AND THE ANTHROPOLOGY OF THE CANYON COUNTRY by John Wesley Powell. Reprint of the U.S. Geological Survey professional paper No. 670. Powell's ethnography dating back to the late 1800s. 30 pages. $4.00

LIGHTFALL AND TIME: FIFTEEN SOUTHWESTERN NATIONAL PARKS by Bennett and Lamb. Paintings and essays about Grand Canyon, Arches, Canyonlands, and 12 other national parks. Informative and inspirational. 64 pages, 15 color plates, 8″ × 8″. $14.95 pb, $24.95 hc

MOUNTAIN LYING DOWN: VIEWS OF THE NORTH RIM by Shoemaker, Euler, and Collier. The biologic, geologic, and cultural history of the North Rim of the Grand Canyon in lay terms. 36 pp. $3.00

RECOLLECTIONS OF PHANTOM RANCH by Elizabeth Simpson. Pocket-sized history of Phantom Ranch, the guest quarters at the bottom of the Canyon. Suggestions for day hikes. 28 pp. $2.50

RIVER RUNNERS OF THE GRAND CANYON by David Lavender. A lively history of river running on the Colorado River as it winds its way through Grand Canyon; 1869 to the present. 75 B/W photographs. 188 pp. $15.00

SKETCH OF GRAND CANYON PREHISTORY by A. Trinkle Jones and Robert Euler. An introduction to the anthropology and archaeology of Grand Canyon written in non-scientific terms. B/W illust. 14 pp. $2.75

TRAIL GUIDES

POCKET-SIZE GUIDES
An informative series of trail guides containing information about the cultural and natural history of the area, as well as trail maps and photographs. 20 – 36 pp. each. $2.50 each

BRIGHT ANGEL	HERMIT
GRANDVIEW	NORTH KAIBAB
HAVASU	SOUTH KAIBAB

GUIDE TO HIKING THE INNER CANYON by Scott Thybony. Descriptions and maps of major trails and routes in Grand Canyon National Park. Includes information on backcountry reservations, safety, and minimum impact hiking. 43 pp. $2.50

VIDEO

RIVER SONG: A NATURAL HISTORY OF THE COLORADO RIVER, narrated by Richard Chamberlain. The river is the lifeblood of the Grand Canyon, yet because of its remoteness it was not explored completely until 1869. Even today it is a challenge to the adventuresome. In this award-winning film we see animals, plants, geology, and the great river itself. 40 minutes. VHS, PAL. $29.95

MAPS

GEOLOGIC MAP OF EASTERN PART OF GRAND CANYON NATIONAL PARK by Breed, Huntoon, and Billingsley. Colorful map graphically shows geologic formations of the Grand Canyon. $6.00

GEOLOGIC MAP OF HURRICANE FAULT ZONE AND VICINITY WESTERN GRAND CANYON, ARIZONA by Huntoon, Billingsley, and Clark, 1981 edition. $6.00

GEOLOGIC MAP OF LOWER GRANITE GORGE AND VICINITY, WESTERN GRAND CANYON, ARIZONA by Huntoon, Billingsley, and Clark, 1982 edition. $6.00

GEOLOGIC MAP OF VULCANS THRONE AND VICINITY, WESTERN GRAND CANYON, ARIZONA by Huntoon, Billingsley, and Clark, 1983 edition. $6.00

FOR CHILDREN

WHERE DO I LOOK? by Franklin and Huey. A child's look at the Grand Canyon provides the opportunity to recognize where we all fit in the scheme of nature. For young children. 42 B/W photographs. 40 pp. $7.50

SCIENTIFIC MONOGRAPHS

AMPHIBIANS AND REPTILES OF THE GRAND CANYON NATIONAL PARK by Donald M. Miller. This study includes 96 tables and illustrations. 224 pp. $11.00

ANNOTATED CHECKLIST OF VASCULAR PLANTS OF GRAND CANYON NATIONAL PARK 1986 by B. Phillips. A. M. Phillips III, and M. A. Schmidt Bernzott. Lists some 1400 species. 80 pp, bibliography, index. $10.00

ARCHAEOLOGY, GEOLOGY AND PALEOBIOLOGY OF STANTON'S CAVE, GRAND CANYON NATIONAL PARK, ARIZONA edited by Robert C. Euler. Presents analyses of archaeological, geological, and biological specimens observed and collected at the cave first visited by Robert Stanton in 1889. 141 pages. $11.00

BIRDS OF THE GRAND CANYON REGION: AN ANNOTATED CHECK LIST (Revised 1984) by Brown, Bennett, Carothers, Haight, Johnson, and Riffey. 50 pages. $10.00

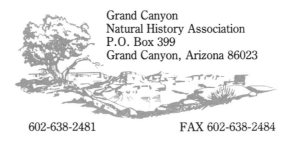

Grand Canyon
Natural History Association
P.O. Box 399
Grand Canyon, Arizona 86023

602-638-2481   FAX 602-638-2484

INDEX

NOTE: "GCNP" stands for "Grand Canyon National Park."

M

Mexico, 25, 38, 42, 73, 101
million years ago/m.y.a. (*see* years ago)
mining (*see* Grand Canyon)
Mojave (*see* Native Americans)
m.y.a./million years ago (*see* years ago)

N

national parks
    idea of, 74, 76
National Park Service
    and river running, 68
    creation of, 79
    how it protects the Canyon, 79–81
    rangers as natural resources, 81
Native Americans
Anasazi, 26–34, 38, 95 (*see also* Anasazi)
    definition of, 25
    Havasupai, 34, 40, 41, 60
    Havasupai pictographs, 87
    Hopi, 34, 39, 40, 48
    Mojave, 47
    Navajo, 26
    of Southwest, 40
    Paiute, 41, 51
    Walapai, 34
Navajo (*see* Native Americans)
Nevills, Norman, 68
Newberry, John Strong, 47
New Mexico, in 1848, 45
New Spain (*see* Mexico)
North America, 24

P

Paiute (*see* Native Americans)
Pattie, James Ohio, 42–43 (*see also* explorers, American)
pictographs, 87
plants, 84, 85, 89, 90, 92–93, 95, 100, 101, 102–103
pottery, 27, 28, 30

Powell, John Wesley, 48–52, 66 (*see also* explorers, American)
prehistorians, 24, 29
public lands, iv
pueblo
    definition of, 28
    Tusayan (*see* Tusayan)
Pueblo Indians, 28

R

rabbit stick, 26
railroads
    Atlantic & Pacific, 58
    first at Grand Canyon, 63
Redwall (*see* geology)
Rio Colorado/Red River (*see* Colorado River)
river runners, 66–68
rock layers (*see* geology)
Roosevelt, Teddy, iii, 77–79

S

sipapu, 34
sleeping circle, 26
Smith, Jedediah, 43 (*see also* explorers, American)
Spain, 39
Spanish explorers (*see* explorers, European)
spear thrower (*see* atlatl)
Stanton, Robert Brewster, 55, 66 (*see also* explorers, American)
stick figures, 24–25
stone tools, 26

T

temples (*see also* erosion)
    Shiva Temple, 52
    Vishnu Temple, 20, 52
    Zoroaster Temple, 20

time
- 1500s, 28, 38
- 1540, 38
- 1776, 40
- 1803, 73
- 1813, 42
- 1829, 43
- 1831, 43
- 1845, 73
- 1848, 45, 73
- 1858, 47, 58
- 1859, 48
- 1864, 75
- 1865, 48
- 1869, 48, 66
- 1870, 53
- 1871, 51
- 1875, 54
- 1880, 52
- 1882, 60
- 1883, 58, 59, 60
- 1884, 58, 60
- 1885, 60
- 1886, 60
- 1889, 66
- 1890, 59
- 1891, 61, 62
- 1892, 61
- 1893, 55
- 1896, 66
- 1897, 62
- 1899, 63
- 1901, 55, 63
- 1902, 65, 68
- 1903, 77
- 1907, 65, 77
- 1908, 78
- 1909, 67
- 1912, 79
- 1916, 79
- 1917, 79
- 1919, 61, 65, 75, 79
- 1923, 60
- 1926, 65
- 1928, 65, 68
- 1929, 54, 65
- 1938, 68
- 1949, 66
- 1974, 80
- 1987, 80
- 2000, 79
- 21st century, 20

Time Travelers, Inc., 9, 13, 14, 20
trails (*see* day hiking and GCNP, trails)
trapping, 42 – 44
tree-ring dating, 31, 33
Tusayan, ancient village of, 29 – 34

U

United States acquires lands from Mexico, 73
U.S. Explorer, 46 – 47

V

village (*see* Tusayan)
volcanoes, 10, 12

W

Walapai (*see* Native Americans)
Wheeler, George M., 51 – 52 (*see also* explorers, American)
White, Georgie, 68
wooden tools, 26 (*see also* hunting)

Y

years ago
- 5 billion (5000 million), 9
- 4.6 billion (4600 million), 11
- 2 billion (2000 million), ii, 15
- 600 million, 16
- 550 million, 15
- 200 million, ii
- 65 million, 10
- 20 million, 16
- 10 million, 13
- 4000, 26
- 1000, 27
- 800, 31, 38
- 500, 38
Yosemite, 75